HBR's 10 Must Reads

UPDATED & EXPANDED

I0112621

Marketing

HBR's 10 Must Reads

HBR's 10 Must Reads are definitive collections of classic ideas, practical advice, and essential thinking from the pages of *Harvard Business Review*. Exploring topics like disruptive innovation, emotional intelligence, and new technology in our ever-evolving world, these books empower any leader to make bold decisions and inspire others.

TITLES INCLUDE:

HBR's 10 Must Reads for New Managers
HBR's 10 Must Reads on Artificial Intelligence
HBR's 10 Must Reads on Building a Great Culture
HBR's 10 Must Reads on Change Management
HBR's 10 Must Reads on Communication
HBR's 10 Must Reads on Data Strategy
HBR's 10 Must Reads on Decision-Making
HBR's 10 Must Reads on Design Thinking
HBR's 10 Must Reads on Emotional Intelligence
HBR's 10 Must Reads on High Performance
HBR's 10 Must Reads on Innovation
HBR's 10 Must Reads on Leadership
HBR's 10 Must Reads on Leading Digital Transformation
HBR's 10 Must Reads on Leading Winning Teams
HBR's 10 Must Reads on Managing People
HBR's 10 Must Reads on Managing Yourself
HBR's 10 Must Reads on Marketing
HBR's 10 Must Reads on Mental Toughness
HBR's 10 Must Reads on Strategy
HBR's 10 Must Reads on Women and Leadership
HBR's 10 Must Reads Boxed Set (6 books)
HBR's 10 Must Reads Ultimate Boxed Set (14 books)

For a full list, visit hbr.org/mustreads.

HBR's 10 Must Reads

UPDATED & EXPANDED

Marketing

Harvard Business Review Press
Boston, Massachusetts

Copyright 2025 Harvard Business Publishing Corporation

Printed in the United States of America

10 9 8 7 6 5 4 3 2 1

The web addresses referenced in this book were live and correct at the time of the book's publication but may be subject to change.

Cataloging-in-Publication data is forthcoming.

ISBN: 979-8-89279-304-9
eISBN: 979-8-89279-305-6

The paper used in this publication meets the requirements of the American National Standard for Permanence of Paper for Publications and Documents in Libraries and Archives Z39.48-1992.

Contents

Marketing Myopia

by Theodore Levitt

Every major industry was once a growth industry. But some that are now riding a wave of growth enthusiasm are very much in the shadow of decline. Others that are thought of as seasoned growth industries have actually stopped growing. In every case, the reason growth is threatened, slowed, or stopped is *not* because the market is saturated. It is because there has been a failure of management.

Fateful Purposes

The failure is at the top. The executives responsible for it, in the last analysis, are those who deal with broad aims and policies. Thus:

- The railroads did not stop growing because the need for passenger and freight transportation declined. That grew. The railroads are in trouble today not because that need was filled by others (cars, trucks, airplanes, and even telephones) but because it was *not* filled by the railroads themselves. They let others take customers away from them because they assumed themselves to be in the railroad business rather than in the transportation business. The reason they defined their industry incorrectly was that they were railroad-oriented instead of transportation-oriented; they were product-oriented instead of customer-oriented.

- Hollywood barely escaped being totally ravished by television. Actually, all the established film companies went through drastic reorganizations. Some simply disappeared. All of them got into trouble not because of TV's inroads but because of their own myopia. As with the railroads, Hollywood defined its business incorrectly. It thought it was in the movie business when it was actually in the entertainment business. "Movies" implied a specific, limited product. This produced a fatuous contentment that from the beginning led producers to view TV as a threat. Hollywood scorned and rejected TV when it should have welcomed it as an opportunity—an opportunity to expand the entertainment business.

Today, TV is a bigger business than the old narrowly defined movie business ever was. Had Hollywood been customer-oriented (providing entertainment) rather than product-oriented (making movies), would it have gone through the fiscal purgatory that it did? I doubt it. What ultimately saved Hollywood and accounted for its resurgence was the wave of new young writers, producers, and directors whose previous successes in television had decimated the old movie companies and toppled the big movie moguls.

There are other, less obvious examples of industries that have been and are now endangering their futures by improperly

Idea in Brief

What business are you *really* in? It's a seemingly obvious question—but one we should all ask *before* demand for our companies' products or services dwindles.

The railroads failed to ask this question—and stopped growing. Why? Not because people no longer needed transportation. And not because other innovations (cars, airplanes) filled transportation needs. Rather, railroads stopped growing because *railroads* didn't move to fill those needs. Their executives incorrectly thought that they were in the railroad business, not the transportation business. They viewed themselves as providing a product instead of serving customers. Too many other industries make the same mistake, putting themselves at risk of obsolescence.

How can you ensure continued growth for your company? Concentrate on meeting customers' needs rather than selling products. Chemical powerhouse DuPont kept a close eye on its customers' most pressing concerns—and deployed its technical know-how to create an ever-expanding array of products that appealed to customers and continuously enlarged its market. If DuPont had merely found more uses for its flagship invention, nylon, the company might not be around today.

defining their purposes. I shall discuss some of them in detail later and analyze the kind of policies that lead to trouble. Right now, it may help to show what a thoroughly customer-oriented management can do to keep a growth industry growing, even after the obvious opportunities have been exhausted, and here there are two examples that have been around for a long time. They are nylon and glass—specifically, E. I. du Pont de Nemours and Company and Corning Glass Works.

Both companies have great technical competence. Their product orientation is unquestioned. But this alone does not explain their success. After all, who was more pridefully product-oriented and product-conscious than the erstwhile New England textile companies that have been so thoroughly massacred? The DuPonts and the Cornings have succeeded not primarily because of their product or research orientation but because they have been thoroughly customer-oriented also. It is constant watchfulness for opportunities to apply their technical know-how to the creation of customer-satisfying uses that accounts for their prodigious output of successful new products. Without a very sophisticated eye on the customer, most of their new products might have been wrong, their sales methods useless.

Aluminum has also continued to be a growth industry, thanks to the efforts of two wartime-created companies that deliberately set about inventing new customer-satisfying uses. Without Kaiser Aluminum & Chemical Corporation and Reynolds Metals Company, the total demand for aluminum today would be vastly less.

Error of analysis

Some may argue that it is foolish to set the railroads off against aluminum or the movies off against glass. Are not aluminum and glass naturally so versatile that the industries are bound to have more growth opportunities than the railroads and the movies? This view commits precisely the error I have been talking about. It defines an industry or a product or a cluster of know-how so narrowly as to guarantee its premature senescence. When we mention "railroads," we should make sure we mean "transportation." As transporters, the railroads still have a good chance for very considerable growth. They are not limited to the railroad business as such (though in my opinion, rail transportation is potentially a much stronger transportation medium than is generally believed).

What the railroads lack is not opportunity but some of the managerial imaginativeness and audacity that made them great. Even an amateur like Jacques Barzun can see what is lacking when he says, "I grieve to see the most advanced physical and social organization of the last century go down in shabby disgrace for lack of the same comprehensive imagination that built it up. [What is lacking is] the will of the companies to survive and to satisfy the public by inventiveness and skill."[1]

Shadow of Obsolescence

It is impossible to mention a single major industry that did not at one time qualify for the magic appellation of "growth industry." In each case, the industry's assumed strength lay in the apparently unchallenged superiority of its product. There appeared to be no effective substitute for it. It was itself a runaway substitute for the product it so triumphantly replaced. Yet one after another of these celebrated industries has come under a shadow. Let us look briefly at a few more of them, this time taking examples that have so far received a little less attention.

Dry cleaning

This was once a growth industry with lavish prospects. In an age of wool garments, imagine being finally able to get them clean safely and easily. The boom was on. Yet here we are 30 years after the boom started, and the industry is in trouble. Where has the competition come from? From a better way of cleaning? No. It has come from synthetic fibers and chemical additives that have cut the need for dry cleaning. But this is only the beginning. Lurking in the wings and ready to make chemical dry cleaning totally obsolete is that powerful magician, ultrasonics.

Electric utilities

This is another one of those supposedly "no substitute" products that has been enthroned on a pedestal of invincible growth.

When the incandescent lamp came along, kerosene lights were finished. Later, the waterwheel and the steam engine were cut to ribbons by the flexibility, reliability, simplicity, and just plain easy availability of electric motors. The prosperity of electric utilities continues to wax extravagant as the home is converted into a museum of electric gadgetry. How can anybody miss by investing in utilities, with no competition, nothing but growth ahead?

But a second look is not quite so comforting. A score of nonutility companies are well advanced toward developing a powerful chemical fuel cell, which could sit in some hidden closet of every home silently ticking off electric power. The electric lines that vulgarize so many neighborhoods would be eliminated. So would the endless demolition of streets and service interruptions during storms. Also on the horizon is solar energy, again pioneered by nonutility companies.

Who says that the utilities have no competition? They may be natural monopolies now, but tomorrow they may be natural deaths. To avoid this prospect, they too will have to develop fuel cells, solar energy, and other power sources. To survive, they themselves will have to plot the obsolescence of what now produces their livelihood.

Grocery stores

Many people find it hard to realize that there ever was a thriving establishment known as the "corner store." The supermarket took over with a powerful effectiveness. Yet the big food chains of the 1930s narrowly escaped being completely wiped out by the aggressive expansion of independent supermarkets. The first genuine supermarket was opened in 1930, in Jamaica, Long Island. By 1933, supermarkets were thriving in California, Ohio,

Pennsylvania, and elsewhere. Yet the established chains pomp-ously ignored them. When they chose to notice them, it was with such derisive descriptions as "cheapy," "horse-and-buggy," "cracker-barrel storekeeping," and "unethical opportunists." The executive of one big chain announced at the time that he found it "hard to believe that people will drive for miles to shop for foods and sacrifice the personal service chains have perfected and to which [the consumer] is accustomed."[2] As late as 1936, the National Wholesale Grocers convention and the New Jersey Retail Grocers Association said there was nothing to fear. They said that the supers' narrow appeal to the price buyer limited the size of their market. They had to draw from miles around. When imitators came, there would be wholesale liqui-dations as volume fell. The high sales of the supers were said to be partly due to their novelty. People wanted convenient neigh-borhood grocers. If the neighborhood stores would "cooperate with their suppliers, pay attention to their costs, and improve their service," they would be able to weather the competition until it blew over.[3]

It never blew over. The chains discovered that survival required going into the supermarket business. This meant the wholesale destruction of their huge investments in corner store sites and in established distribution and merchandising meth-ods. The companies with "the courage of their convictions" reso-lutely stuck to the corner store philosophy. They kept their pride but lost their shirts.

A self-deceiving cycle

But memories are short. For example, it is hard for people who today confidently hail the twin messiahs of electronics and chemicals to see how things could possibly go wrong with these galloping industries. They probably also cannot see how a reasonably sensible businessperson could have been as myopic as the famous Boston millionaire who early in the twentieth century unintentionally sentenced his heirs to poverty by stipulating that his entire estate be forever invested exclusively in electric streetcar securities. His posthumous declaration, "There will always be a big demand for efficient urban transportation" is no consolation to his heirs, who sustain life by pumping gasoline at automobile filling stations.

Yet, in a casual survey I took among a group of intelligent business executives, nearly half agreed that it would be hard to hurt their heirs by tying their estates forever to the electronics industry. When I then confronted them with the Boston streetcar example, they chorused unanimously, "That's different!" But is it? Is not the basic situation identical?

In truth, *there is no such thing as a growth industry,* I believe. There are only companies organized and operated to create and capitalize on growth opportunities. Industries that assume themselves to be riding some automatic growth escalator invariably descend into stagnation. The history of every dead and dying "growth" industry shows a self-deceiving cycle of bountiful expansion and undetected decay. There are four conditions that usually guarantee this cycle:

1. The belief that growth is assured by an expanding and more affluent population;

2. The belief that there is no competitive substitute for the industry's major product;

3. Too much faith in mass production and in the advantages of rapidly declining unit costs as output rises;

4. Preoccupation with a product that lends itself to carefully controlled scientific experimentation, improvement, and manufacturing cost reduction.

I should like now to examine each of these conditions in some detail. To build my case as boldly as possible, I shall illustrate the points with reference to three industries: petroleum, automobiles, and electronics. I'll focus on petroleum in particular, because it spans more years and more vicissitudes. Not only do these three industries have excellent reputations with the general public and also enjoy the confidence of sophisticated investors, but their managements have become known for progressive thinking in areas like financial control, product research, and management training. If obsolescence can cripple even these industries, it can happen anywhere.

Population Myth

The belief that profits are assured by an expanding and more affluent population is dear to the heart of every industry. It takes the edge off the apprehensions everybody understandably feels about the future. If consumers are multiplying and also buying more of your product or service, you can face the future with considerably more comfort than if the market were shrinking. An expanding market keeps the manufacturer from having to think very hard or imaginatively. If thinking is an intellectual response to a problem, then the absence of a problem leads to the absence of thinking. If your product has an automatically expanding market, then you will not give much thought to how to expand it.

One of the most interesting examples of this is provided by the petroleum industry. Probably our oldest growth industry, it has an enviable record. While there are some current concerns about its growth rate, the industry itself tends to be optimistic.

But I believe it can be demonstrated that it is undergoing a fundamental yet typical change. It is not only ceasing to be a growth industry but may actually be a declining one, relative to other businesses. Although there is widespread unawareness of this fact, it is conceivable that in time, the oil industry may find itself in much the same position of retrospective glory that the railroads are now in. Despite its pioneering work in developing and applying the present-value method of investment evaluation, in employee relations, and in working with developing countries, the petroleum business is a distressing example of how complacency and wrongheadedness can stubbornly convert opportunity into near disaster.

One of the characteristics of this and other industries that have believed very strongly in the beneficial consequences of an expanding population, while at the same time having a generic product for which there has appeared to be no competitive substitute, is that the individual companies have sought to outdo their competitors by improving on what they are already doing. This makes sense, of course, if one assumes that sales are tied to the country's population strings, because the customer can compare products only on a feature-by-feature basis. I believe it is significant, for example, that not since John D. Rockefeller sent free kerosene lamps to China has the oil industry done anything really outstanding to create a demand for its product. Not even in product improvement has it showered itself with eminence. The greatest single improvement—the development of tetraethyl lead—came from outside the industry, specifically from General Motors and DuPont. The big contributions made by the industry itself are confined to the technology of oil exploration, oil production, and oil refining.

Asking for trouble

In other words, the petroleum industry's efforts have focused on improving the *efficiency* of getting and making its product, not really on improving the generic product or its marketing. Moreover, its chief product has continually been defined in the narrowest possible terms—namely, gasoline, not energy, fuel, or transportation. This attitude has helped assure that:

- Major improvements in gasoline quality tend not to originate in the oil industry. The development of superior alternative fuels also comes from outside the oil industry, as will be shown later.

- Major innovations in automobile fuel marketing come from small, new oil companies that are not primarily preoccupied with production or refining. These are the companies that have been responsible for the rapidly expanding multipump gasoline stations, with their successful emphasis on large and clean layouts, rapid and efficient driveway service, and quality gasoline at low prices.

Thus, the oil industry is asking for trouble from outsiders. Sooner or later, in this land of hungry investors and entrepreneurs, a threat is sure to come. The possibility of this will become more apparent when we turn to the next dangerous belief of many managements. For the sake of continuity, because this second belief is tied closely to the first, I shall continue with the same example.

The idea of indispensability

The petroleum industry is pretty much convinced that there is no competitive substitute for its major product, gasoline—or, if there is, that it will continue to be a derivative of crude oil, such as diesel fuel or kerosene jet fuel.

There is a lot of automatic wishful thinking in this assumption. The trouble is that most refining companies own huge amounts of crude oil reserves. These have value only if there is a market for products into which oil can be converted. Hence the tenacious belief in the continuing competitive superiority of automobile fuels made from crude oil.

This idea persists despite all historic evidence against it. The evidence not only shows that oil has never been a superior product for any purpose for very long but also that the oil industry has never really been a growth industry. Rather, it has been a succession of different businesses that have gone through the usual historic cycles of growth, maturity, and decay. The industry's overall survival is owed to a series of miraculous escapes from total obsolescence, of last-minute and unexpected reprieves from total disaster reminiscent of the perils of Pauline.

The perils of petroleum

To illustrate, I shall sketch in only the main episodes. First, crude oil was largely a patent medicine. But even before that fad ran out, demand was greatly expanded by the use of oil in kerosene lamps. The prospect of lighting the world's lamps gave rise to an extravagant promise of growth. The prospects were similar to those the industry now holds for gasoline in other parts of the world. It can hardly wait for the underdeveloped nations to get a car in every garage.

In the days of the kerosene lamp, the oil companies competed with each other and against gaslight by trying to improve the illuminating characteristics of kerosene. Then suddenly the impossible happened. Edison invented a light that was totally nondependent on crude oil. Had it not been for the growing use of kerosene in space heaters, the incandescent lamp would have completely finished oil as a growth industry at that time. Oil would have been good for little else than axle grease.

Then disaster and reprieve struck again. Two great innovations occurred, neither originating in the oil industry. First, the successful development of coal-burning domestic central-heating systems made the space heater obsolete. While the industry reeled, along came its most magnificent boost yet: the internal combustion engine, also invented by outsiders. Then, when the prodigious expansion for gasoline finally began to level off in the 1920s, along came the miraculous escape of the central oil heater. Once again, the escape was provided by an outsider's invention and development. And when that market weakened, wartime demand for aviation fuel came to the rescue. After the war, the expansion of civilian aviation, the dieselization of railroads, and the explosive demand for cars and trucks kept the industry's growth in high gear.

Meanwhile, centralized oil heating—whose boom potential had only recently been proclaimed—ran into severe competition from natural gas. While the oil companies themselves owned the gas that now competed with their oil, the industry did not originate the natural gas revolution, nor has it to this day greatly profited from its gas ownership. The gas revolution was made by newly formed transmission companies that marketed the product with an aggressive ardor. They started a magnificent new industry, first against the advice and then against the resistance of the oil companies.

By all the logic of the situation, the oil companies themselves should have made the gas revolution. They not only owned the gas, they also were the only people experienced in handling, scrubbing, and using it and the only people experienced in pipeline technology and transmission. They also understood heating problems. But, partly because they knew that natural gas would compete with their own sale of heating oil, the oil companies pooh-poohed the potential of gas. The revolution was finally started by oil pipeline executives who, unable to persuade their own companies to go into gas, quit and organized the spectacularly successful gas transmission companies. Even after their success became painfully evident to the oil companies, the latter did not go into gas transmission. The multibillion-dollar business that should have been theirs went to others. As in the past, the industry was blinded by its narrow preoccupation with a specific product and the value of its reserves. It paid little or no attention to its customers' basic needs and preferences.

The postwar years have not witnessed any change. Immediately after World War II, the oil industry was greatly encouraged about its future by the rapid increase in demand for its traditional line of products. In 1950, most companies projected annual rates of domestic expansion of around 6% through at least 1975. Though the ratio of crude oil reserves to demand in the free world was about 20 to 1, with 10 to 1 being usually considered a reasonable working ratio in the United States, booming demand sent oil explorers searching for more without sufficient regard to what the future really promised. In 1952, they "hit" in the Middle East; the ratio skyrocketed to 42 to 1. If gross additions to reserves continue at the average rate of the past five years (37 billion barrels annually), then by 1970, the reserve ratio will be up to 45 to 1. This abundance of oil has weakened crude and product prices all over the world.

An uncertain future

Management cannot find much consolation today in the rapidly expanding petrochemical industry, another oil-using idea that did not originate in the leading firms. The total U.S. production of petrochemicals is equivalent to about 2% (by volume) of the demand for all petroleum products. Although the petrochemical industry is now expected to grow by about 10% per year, this will not offset other drains on the growth of crude oil consumption. Furthermore, while petrochemical products are many and growing, it is important to remember that there are nonpetroleum sources of the basic raw material, such as coal. Besides, a lot of plastics can be produced with relatively little oil. A 50,000-barrel-per-day oil refinery is now considered the absolute minimum size for efficiency. But a 5,000-barrel-per-day chemical plant is a giant operation.

Oil has never been a continuously strong growth industry. It has grown by fits and starts, always miraculously saved by innovations and developments not of its own making. The reason it has not grown in a smooth progression is that each time it thought it had a superior product safe from the possibility of competitive substitutes, the product turned out to be inferior and notoriously subject to obsolescence. Until now, gasoline (for motor fuel, anyhow) has escaped this fate. But, as we shall see later, it too may be on its last legs.

The point of all this is that there is no guarantee against product obsolescence. If a company's own research does not make a product obsolete, another's will. Unless an industry is especially lucky, as oil has been until now, it can easily go down in a sea of red figures— just as the railroads have, as the buggy whip manufacturers have, as the corner grocery chains have, as most of the big movie companies have, and, indeed, as many other industries have.

The best way for a firm to be lucky is to make its own luck. That requires knowing what makes a business successful. One of the greatest enemies of this knowledge is mass production.

Production Pressures

Mass production industries are impelled by a great drive to produce all they can. The prospect of steeply declining unit costs as output rises is more than most companies can usually resist. The profit possibilities look spectacular. All effort focuses on production. The result is that marketing gets neglected.

John Kenneth Galbraith contends that just the opposite occurs.[4] Output is so prodigious that all effort concentrates on trying to get rid of it. He says this accounts for singing commercials, the desecration of the countryside with advertising signs, and other wasteful and vulgar practices. Galbraith has a finger on something real, but he misses the strategic point. Mass production does indeed generate great pressure to "move" the product. But what usually gets emphasized is selling, not marketing. Marketing, a more sophisticated and complex process, gets ignored.

The difference between marketing and selling is more than semantic. Selling focuses on the needs of the seller, marketing on the needs of the buyer. Selling is preoccupied with the seller's need to convert the product into cash, marketing with the idea of satisfying the needs of the customer by means of the product and the whole cluster of things associated with creating, delivering, and, finally, consuming it.

In some industries, the enticements of full mass production have been so powerful that top management in effect has told the sales department, "You get rid of it; we'll worry about profits." By contrast, a truly marketing-minded firm tries to create value-satisfying goods and services that consumers will want to buy. What it offers for sale includes not only the generic product or service but also how it is made available to the customer, in what form, when, under what conditions, and at what terms of trade. Most important, what it offers for sale is determined not by the seller but by the buyer. The seller takes cues from the buyer in such a way that the product becomes a consequence of the marketing effort, not vice versa.

A lag in Detroit

This may sound like an elementary rule of business, but that does not keep it from being violated wholesale. It is certainly more violated than honored. Take the automobile industry.

Here mass production is most famous, most honored, and has the greatest impact on the entire society. The industry has hitched its fortune to the relentless requirements of the annual model change, a policy that makes customer orientation an especially urgent necessity. Consequently, the auto companies annually spend millions of dollars on consumer research. But the fact that the new compact cars are selling so well in their first year indicates that Detroit's vast researches have for a long time failed to reveal what customers really wanted. Detroit was not convinced that people wanted anything different from what they had been getting until it lost millions of customers to other small-car manufacturers.

How could this unbelievable lag behind consumer wants have been perpetuated for so long? Why didn't research reveal consumer preferences before consumers' buying decisions themselves revealed the facts? Isn't that what consumer research is for—to find out before the fact what is going to happen? The answer is that Detroit never really researched customers' wants. It only researched their preferences between the kinds of things it had already decided to offer them. For Detroit is mainly product-oriented, not customer-oriented. To the extent that the customer is recognized as having needs that the manufacturer should try to satisfy, Detroit usually acts as if the job can be done entirely by product changes. Occasionally, attention gets paid to financing, too, but that is done more in order to sell than to enable the customer to buy.

As for taking care of other customer needs, there is not enough being done to write about. The areas of the greatest unsatisfied needs are ignored or, at best, get stepchild attention. These are at the point of sale and on the matter of automotive repair and maintenance. Detroit views these problem areas as being of secondary importance. That is underscored by the fact that the retailing and servicing ends of this industry are neither owned and operated nor controlled by the manufacturers. Once the car is produced, things are pretty much in the dealer's inadequate hands. Illustrative of Detroit's arm's-length attitude is the fact that, while servicing holds enormous sales-stimulating, profit-building opportunities, only 57 of Chevrolet's 7,000 dealers provide night maintenance service.

Motorists repeatedly express their dissatisfaction with servicing and their apprehensions about buying cars under the present selling setup. The anxieties and problems they encounter during the auto buying and maintenance processes are probably more intense and widespread today than many years ago. Yet the automobile companies do not seem to listen to or take their cues from the anguished consumer. If they do listen, it must be through the filter of their own preoccupation with production. The marketing effort is still viewed as a necessary consequence of the product—not vice versa, as it should be. That is the legacy of mass production, with its parochial view that profit resides essentially in low-cost full production.

What Ford put first

The profit lure of mass production obviously has a place in the plans and strategy of business management, but it must always *follow* hard thinking about the customer. This is one of the most important lessons we can learn from the contradictory behavior of Henry Ford. In a sense, Ford was both the most brilliant and the most senseless marketer in American history. He was senseless because he refused to give the customer anything but a black car. He was brilliant because he fashioned a production system designed to fit market needs. We habitually celebrate him for the wrong reason: for his production genius. His real genius was marketing. We think he was able to cut his selling price and therefore sell millions of $500 cars because his invention of the assembly line had reduced the costs. Actually, he invented the assembly line because he had concluded that at $500 he could sell millions of cars. Mass production was the *result,* not the cause, of his low prices.

Ford emphasized this point repeatedly, but a nation of production-oriented business managers refuses to hear the great lesson he taught. Here is his operating philosophy as he expressed it succinctly:

Our policy is to reduce the price, extend the operations, and improve the article. You will notice that the reduction of price comes first. We have never considered any costs as fixed. Therefore we first reduce the price to the point where we believe more sales will result. Then we go ahead and try to make the prices. We do not bother about the costs. The new price forces the costs down. The more usual way is to take the costs and then determine the price; and although that method may be scientific in the narrow sense, it is not scientific in the broad sense, because what earthly use is it to know the cost if it tells you that you cannot manufacture at a price at which the article can be sold? But more to the point is the fact that, although one may calculate what a cost is, and of course all of our costs are carefully calculated, no one knows what a cost ought to be. One of the ways of discovering . . . is to name a price so low as to force everybody in the place to the highest point of efficiency. The low price makes everybody dig for profits. We make more discoveries concerning manufacturing and selling under this forced method than by any method of leisurely investigation.[5]

Product provincialism

The tantalizing profit possibilities of low unit production costs may be the most seriously self-deceiving attitude that can afflict a company, particularly a "growth" company, where an apparently assured expansion of demand already tends to undermine a proper concern for the importance of marketing and the customer. The usual result of this narrow preoccupation with so-called concrete matters is that instead of growing, the industry declines. It usually means that the product fails to adapt to the constantly changing patterns of consumer needs and tastes, to new and modified marketing institutions and practices, or to product developments in competing or complementary industries. The industry has its eyes so firmly on its own specific product that it does not see how it is being made obsolete.

The classic example of this is the buggy whip industry. No amount of product improvement could stave off its death sentence. But had the industry defined itself as being in the transportation business rather than in the buggy whip business, it might have survived. It would have done what survival always entails—that is, change. Even if it had only defined its business as providing a stimulant or catalyst to an energy source, it might have survived by becoming a manufacturer of, say, fan belts or air cleaners.

What may someday be a still more classic example is, again, the oil industry. Having let others steal marvelous opportunities from it (including natural gas, as already mentioned; missile fuels; and jet engine lubricants), one would expect it to have taken steps never to let that happen again. But this is not the case. We are now seeing extraordinary new developments in fuel systems specifically designed to power automobiles. Not only are these developments concentrated in firms outside the petroleum industry, but petroleum is almost systematically ignoring them, securely content in its wedded bliss to oil. It is the story of the kerosene lamp versus the incandescent lamp all over again. Oil is trying to improve hydrocarbon fuels rather than develop *any* fuels best suited to the needs of their users, whether or not made in different ways and with different raw materials from oil. Here are some things that nonpetroleum companies are working on:

- More than a dozen such firms now have advanced working models of energy systems, which, when perfected, will replace the internal combustion engine and eliminate the demand for gasoline. The superior merit of each of these systems is their elimination of frequent, time-consuming, and irritating refueling stops. Most of these systems are fuel cells designed to create electrical energy directly from chemicals without combustion. Most of them use chemicals that are not derived from oil—generally, hydrogen and oxygen.

- Several other companies have advanced models of electric storage batteries designed to power automobiles. One of these is an aircraft producer that is working jointly with several electric utility companies. The latter hope to use off-peak generating capacity to supply overnight plug-in battery regeneration. Another company, also using the battery approach, is a medium-sized electronics firm with extensive small-battery experience that it developed in connection with its work on hearing aids. It is collaborating with an automobile manufacturer. Recent improvements arising from the need for high-powered miniature power storage plants in rockets have put us within reach of a relatively small battery capable of withstanding great overloads or surges of power. Germanium diode applications and batteries using sintered plate and nickel cadmium techniques promise to make a revolution in our energy sources.

• Solar energy conversion systems are also getting increasing attention. One usually cautious Detroit auto executive recently ventured that solar-powered cars might be common by 1980.

As for the oil companies, they are more or less "watching developments," as one research director put it to me. A few are doing a bit of research on fuel cells, but this research is almost always confined to developing cells powered by hydrocarbon chemicals. None of them is enthusiastically researching fuel cells, batteries, or solar power plants. None of them is spending a fraction as much on research in these profoundly important areas as it is on the usual run-of-the-mill things like reducing combustion chamber deposits in gasoline engines. One major integrated petroleum company recently took a tentative look at the fuel cell and concluded that although "the companies actively working on it indicate a belief in ultimate success . . . the timing and magnitude of its impact are too remote to warrant recognition in our forecasts."

One might, of course, ask, Why should the oil companies do anything different? Would not chemical fuel cells, batteries, or solar energy kill the present product lines? The answer is that they would indeed, and that is precisely the reason for the oil firms' having to develop these power units before their competitors do, so they will not be companies without an industry.

Management might be more likely to do what is needed for its own preservation if it thought of itself as being in the energy business. But even that will not be enough if it persists in imprisoning itself in the narrow grip of its tight product orientation. It has to think of itself as taking care of customer needs, not finding, refining, or even selling oil. Once it genuinely thinks of its business as taking care of people's transportation needs, nothing can stop it from creating its own extravagantly profitable growth.

Creative destruction

Since words are cheap and deeds are dear, it may be appropriate to indicate what this kind of thinking involves and leads to. Let us start at the beginning: the customer. It can be shown that motorists strongly dislike the bother, delay, and experience of buying gasoline. People actually do not buy gasoline. They cannot see it, taste it, feel it, appreciate it, or really test it. What they buy is the right to continue driving their cars. The gas station is like a tax collector to whom people are compelled to pay a periodic toll as the price of using their cars. This makes the gas station a basically unpopular institution. It can never be made popular or pleasant, only less unpopular, less unpleasant.

Reducing its unpopularity completely means eliminating it. Nobody likes a tax collector, not even a pleasantly cheerful one. Nobody likes to interrupt a trip to buy a phantom product, not even from a handsome Adonis or a seductive Venus. Hence, companies that are working on exotic fuel substitutes that will eliminate the need for frequent refueling are heading directly into the outstretched arms of the irritated motorist. They are riding a wave of inevitability, not because they are creating something that is technologically superior or more sophisticated but because they are satisfying a powerful customer need. They are also eliminating noxious odors and air pollution.

Once the petroleum companies recognize the customer-satisfying logic of what another power system can do, they will see that they have no more choice about working on an efficient, long-lasting fuel (or some way of delivering present fuels without bothering the motorist) than the big food chains had a choice about going into the supermarket business or the vacuum tube companies had a choice about making semiconductors. For their own good, the oil firms will have to destroy their own highly profitable assets. No amount of wishful thinking can save them from the necessity of engaging in this form of "creative destruction."

I phrase the need as strongly as this because I think management must make quite an effort to break itself loose from conventional ways. It is all too easy in this day and age for a company or industry to let its sense of purpose become dominated by the economies of full production and to develop a dangerously lopsided product orientation. In short, if management lets itself drift, it invariably drifts in the direction of thinking of itself as producing goods and services, not customer satisfactions. While it probably will not descend to the depths of telling its salespeople, "You get rid of it; we'll worry about profits," it can, without knowing it, be practicing precisely that formula for withering decay. The historic fate of one growth industry after another has been its suicidal product provincialism.

Dangers of R&D

Another big danger to a firm's continued growth arises when top management is wholly transfixed by the profit possibilities of technical research and development. To illustrate, I shall turn first to a new industry—electronics—and then return once more to the oil companies. By comparing a fresh example with a familiar one, I hope to emphasize the prevalence and insidiousness of a hazardous way of thinking.

Marketing shortchanged

In the case of electronics, the greatest danger that faces the glamorous new companies in this field is not that they do not pay enough attention to research and development but that they pay too much attention to it. And the fact that the fastest-growing electronics firms owe their eminence to their heavy emphasis on technical research is completely beside the point. They have vaulted to affluence on a sudden crest of unusually strong general receptiveness to new technical ideas. Also, their success has been shaped in the virtually guaranteed market of military subsidies and by military orders that in many cases actually preceded the existence of facilities to make the products. Their expansion has, in other words, been almost totally devoid of marketing effort.

Thus, they are growing up under conditions that come dangerously close to creating the illusion that a superior product will sell itself. It is not surprising that, having created a successful company by making a superior product, management continues to be oriented toward the product rather than the people who consume it. It develops the philosophy that continued growth is a matter of continued product innovation and improvement.

A number of other factors tend to strengthen and sustain this belief:

1. Because electronic products are highly complex and sophisticated, managements become top-heavy with engineers and scientists. This creates a selective bias in favor of research and production at the expense of marketing. The organization tends to view itself as making things rather than as satisfying customer needs. Marketing gets

treated as a residual activity, "something else" that must be done once the vital job of product creation and production is completed.

2. To this bias in favor of product research, development, and production is added the bias in favor of dealing with controllable variables. Engineers and scientists are at home in the world of concrete things like machines, test tubes, production lines, and even balance sheets. The abstractions to which they feel kindly are those that are testable or manipulatable in the laboratory or, if not testable, then functional, such as Euclid's axioms. In short, the managements of the new glamour-growth companies tend to favor business activities that lend themselves to careful study, experimentation, and control—the hard, practical realities of the lab, the shop, and the books.

What gets shortchanged are the realities of the *market*. Consumers are unpredictable, varied, fickle, stupid, shortsighted, stubborn, and generally bothersome. This is not what the engineer managers say, but deep down in their consciousness, it is what they believe. And this accounts for their concentration on what they know and what they can control—namely, product research, engineering, and production. The emphasis on production becomes particularly attractive when the product can be made at declining unit costs. There is no more inviting way of making money than by running the plant full blast.

The top-heavy science-engineering-production orientation of so many electronics companies works reasonably well today because they are pushing into new frontiers in which the armed services have pioneered virtually assured markets. The companies are in the felicitous position of having to fill, not find, markets, of not having to discover what the customer needs and wants but of having the customer voluntarily come forward with specific new product demands. If a team of consultants had been assigned specifically to design a business situation calculated to prevent the emergence and development of a customer-oriented marketing viewpoint, it could not have produced anything better than the conditions just described.

Stepchild treatment

The oil industry is a stunning example of how science, technology, and mass production can divert an entire group of companies from their main task. To the extent the consumer is studied at all (which is not much), the focus is forever on getting information that is designed to help the oil companies improve what they are now doing. They try to discover more convincing advertising themes, more effective sales promotional drives, what the market shares of the various companies are, what people like or dislike about service station dealers and oil companies, and so forth. Nobody seems as interested in probing deeply into the basic human needs that the industry might be trying to satisfy as in probing into the basic properties of the raw material that the companies work with in trying to deliver customer satisfactions.

Basic questions about customers and markets seldom get asked. The latter occupy a stepchild status. They are recognized as existing, as having to be taken care of, but not worth very much real thought or dedicated attention. No oil company gets as excited about the customers in its own backyard as about the oil in the Sahara Desert. Nothing illustrates better the neglect of marketing than its treatment in the industry press.

The centennial issue of the *American Petroleum Institute Quarterly,* published in 1959 to celebrate the discovery of oil in

Titusville, Pennsylvania, contained 21 feature articles proclaiming the industry's greatness. Only one of these talked about its achievements in marketing, and that was only a pictorial record of how service station architecture has changed. The issue also contained a special section on "New Horizons," which was devoted to showing the magnificent role oil would play in America's future. Every reference was ebulliently optimistic, never implying once that oil might have some hard competition. Even the reference to atomic energy was a cheerful catalog of how oil would help make atomic energy a success. There was not a single apprehension that the oil industry's affluence might be threatened or a suggestion that one "new horizon" might include new and better ways of serving oil's present customers.

But the most revealing example of the stepchild treatment that marketing gets is still another special series of short articles on "The Revolutionary Potential of Electronics." Under that heading, this list of articles appeared in the table of contents:

- "In the Search for Oil"

- "In Production Operations"

- "In Refinery Processes"

- "In Pipeline Operations"

Significantly, every one of the industry's major functional areas is listed, *except* marketing. Why? Either it is believed that electronics holds no revolutionary potential for petroleum marketing (which is palpably wrong), or the editors forgot to discuss marketing (which is more likely and illustrates its stepchild status).

The order in which the four functional areas are listed also betrays the alienation of the oil industry from the consumer. The industry is implicitly defined as beginning with the search for oil and ending with its distribution from the refinery. But the truth is, it seems to me, that the industry begins with the needs of the customer for its products. From that primal position its definition moves steadily back stream to areas of progressively lesser importance until it finally comes to rest at the search for oil.

The beginning and end

The view that an industry is a customer-satisfying process, not a goods-producing process, is vital for all businesspeople to understand. An industry begins with the customer and their needs, not with a patent, a raw material, or a selling skill. Given the customer's needs, the industry develops backward, first concerning itself with the physical *delivery* of customer satisfactions. Then it moves back further to *creating* the things by which these satisfactions are in part achieved. How these materials are created is a matter of indifference to the customer, hence the particular form of manufacturing, processing, or what have you cannot be considered as a vital aspect of the industry. Finally, the industry moves back still further to *finding* the raw materials necessary for making its products.

The irony of some industries oriented toward technical research and development is that the scientists who occupy the high executive positions are totally unscientific when it comes to defining their companies' overall needs and purposes. They violate the first two rules of the scientific method: being aware of and defining their companies' problems and then developing testable hypotheses about solving them. They are scientific only about the convenient things, such as laboratory and product experiments.

The customer (and the satisfaction of their deepest needs) is not considered to be "the problem"—not because there is any certain belief that no such problem exists but because an organizational lifetime has conditioned management to look in the opposite direction. Marketing is a stepchild. I do not mean that selling is ignored. Far from it. But selling, again, is not marketing. As already pointed out, selling concerns itself with the tricks and techniques of getting people to exchange their cash for your product. It is not concerned with the values that the exchange is all about. And it does not, as marketing invariably does, view the entire business process as consisting of a tightly integrated effort to discover, create, arouse, and satisfy customer needs. The customer is somebody "out there" who, with proper cunning, can be separated from their loose change.

Actually, not even selling gets much attention in some technologically minded firms. Because there is a virtually guaranteed market for the abundant flow of their new products, they do not actually know what a real market is. It is as if they lived in a planned economy, moving their products routinely from factory to retail outlet. Their successful concentration on products tends to convince them of the soundness of what they have been doing, and they fail to see the gathering clouds over the market.

. . .

Less than 75 years ago, American railroads enjoyed a fierce loyalty among astute Wall Streeters. European monarchs invested in them heavily. Eternal wealth was thought to be the benediction for anybody who could scrape together a few thousand dollars to put into rail stocks. No other form of transportation could compete with the railroads in speed, flexibility, durability, economy, and growth potentials.

As Jacques Barzun put it, "By the turn of the century it was an institution, an image of man, a tradition, a code of honor, a source of poetry, a nursery of boyhood desires, a sublimest of toys, and the most solemn machine—next to the funeral hearse—that marks the epochs in man's life."[6]

Even after the advent of automobiles, trucks, and airplanes, the railroad tycoons remained imperturbably self-confident. If you had told them 60 years ago that in 30 years they would be flat on their backs, broke, and pleading for government subsidies, they would have thought you totally demented. Such a future was simply not considered possible. It was not even a discussable subject, or an askable question, or a matter that any sane person would consider worth speculating about. Yet a lot of "insane" notions now have matter-of-fact acceptance—for example, the idea of 100-ton tubes of metal moving smoothly through the air 20,000 feet above the earth, loaded with 100 sane and solid citizens casually drinking martinis—and they have dealt cruel blows to the railroads.

What specifically must other companies do to avoid this fate? What does customer orientation involve? These questions have in part been answered by the preceding examples and analysis. It would take another article to show in detail what is required for specific industries. In any case, it should be obvious that building an effective customer-oriented company involves far more than good intentions or promotional tricks; it involves profound matters of human organization and leadership. For the present, let me merely suggest what appear to be some general requirements.

The visceral feel of greatness

Obviously, the company has to do what survival demands. It has to adapt to the requirements of the market, and it has to do it sooner rather than later. But mere survival is a so-so aspiration. Anybody can survive in some way or other, even the skid row bum. The trick is to survive gallantly, to feel the surging impulse of commercial mastery: not just to experience the sweet smell of success but to have the visceral feel of entrepreneurial greatness. No organization can achieve greatness without a vigorous leader who is driven onward by a pulsating *will to succeed.* A leader has to have a vision of grandeur, a vision that can produce eager followers in vast numbers. In business, the followers are the customers.

In order to produce these customers, the entire corporation must be viewed as a customer-creating and customer-satisfying organism. Management must think of itself not as producing products but as providing customer-creating value satisfactions. It must push this idea (and everything it means and requires) into every nook and cranny of the organization. It has to do this continuously and with the kind of flair that excites and stimulates the people in it. Otherwise, the company will be merely a series of pigeonholed parts, with no consolidating sense of purpose or direction.

In short, the organization must learn to think of itself not as producing goods or services but as *buying customers,* as doing the things that will make people *want* to do business with it. And the chief executive has the inescapable responsibility for creating this environment, this viewpoint, this attitude, this aspiration. The chief executive must set the company's style, its direction, and its goals. This means knowing precisely where they want to go and making sure the whole organization is enthusiastically aware of where that is. This is a first requisite of leadership, for *unless a leader knows where they are going, any road will take them there.*

If any road is OK, the chief executive might as well pack their attaché case and go fishing. If an organization does not know or care where it is going, it does not need to advertise that fact with a ceremonial figurehead. Everybody will notice it soon enough.

Reprinted from *Harvard Business Review*, July–August 2004.
Reprint R0407L. Originally published July–August 1960

2

Net Promoter 3.0

by Fred Reichheld, Darci Darnell, and Maureen Burns

O n a scale from 0 to 10, how likely would you be to recommend our company to a friend?

As a consumer, you've probably encountered this sort of question dozens of times—after an online purchase, at the end of a customer service interaction, or even after a hospital stay. And if you work at one of the thousands of companies that ask this question of their customers, you're familiar with the Net Promoter System (NPS), which Reichheld invented and first wrote about in HBR almost 20 years ago. (See "The One Number You Need to Grow," December 2003.) Since then, NPS has spread rapidly around the world. It has become the predominant customer success framework—used today by two-thirds of the *Fortune* 1000. Why has it been embraced so enthusiastically? Because it solves a vital challenge that our financial systems fail to address. Financials can easily tell us when we have extracted $1 million from our customers' wallets, but they can't tell us when our work has improved customers' lives.

That's the objective of NPS. It gauges how consistently a firm turns customers into advocates, by tracking and analyzing three segments: *promoters*, customers who are so pleased with their experience that they recommend your brand to others; *passives*, customers who feel they got what they paid for but nothing more and who are not loyal assets with lasting value; and *detractors*, customers who are disappointed with their experience and harm the firm's growth and reputation. Promoters give a score of 9 or 10, passives a 7 or 8, and detractors a 6 or less. To calculate your firm's overall Net Promoter Score, you subtract the percentage of your customers who are detractors from the percentage who are promoters.

While that arithmetic might seem simplistic, the full system is intended to inspire teams to deliver experiences that are not merely satisfactory but remarkable. When customers feel cared for, they come back for more and bring their friends.

The power of customer advocacy is evidenced by the remarkable success of NPS leaders. Consider the 11 public firms highlighted in Reichheld's most recent book, *The Ultimate Question 2.0*. Over the past decade their median total shareholder return was five times the U.S. median (for public companies with revenues of more than $500 million as of 2010). Those results motivated more firms to track their Net Promoter Scores—and some to report them to investors.

Unfortunately, self-reported scores and misinterpretations of the NPS framework have sown confusion and diminished its credibility. Inexperienced practitioners abused it by doing things like linking Net Promoter Scores to bonuses for frontline employees, which made them care more about their scores than about learning to better serve customers. Many firms amplify the problem by publicly reporting their scores to investors with

Idea in Brief

The Problem

The widely popular Net Promoter System has been misused and misunderstood.

The Cause

Firms corrupted a valuable metric, the Net Promoter Score, by making it into a target and reporting unaudited vanity statistics that hurt the credibility and usefulness of NPS.

The Solution

An accounting-based counterpart for the Net Promoter Score, *earned growth rate*, provides firms with a clear, data-driven connection between customer success, repeat and expanded purchases, recommendations, a positive company culture, and business results.

no explanation of the process used to generate them and no safeguards to prevent pleading ("I'll lose my job if you don't rate me a 10"), bribery ("We'll give you free oil changes for a 10"), and manipulation ("We never send surveys to customers whose claim was denied"). No details are provided about which customers (and how many) were surveyed, their response rates, or whether the survey was triggered by a specific transaction. Reports rarely mention whether the research was performed by a reliable third-party expert using double-blind methodology. In other words, some firms have turned Net Promoter Scores into vanity statistics that damage the credibility of NPS.

Over time we realized that the only way to make the system work better was to develop a complementary metric that drew on accounting results, not on surveys. We needed one that would illuminate the quality (and the likely profitability) of a firm's growth. It had to be based on audited revenues from all customers, not just on a potentially biased sample of survey responses, so that it would be far more resistant to gaming, coaching, pleading, and the response biases that plague the results of nonanonymized surveys. We're confident we've successfully developed that metric.

In this article we introduce *earned growth* as the accounting-based counterpart for the Net Promoter Score, one that will reinforce the effectiveness of NPS, providing firms with a clear, data-driven connection between customer success, repeat and expanded purchases, word-of-mouth recommendations, a positive company culture, and business results.

The Origin of Earned Growth

The superior economics of companies with high Net Promoter Scores prove that generating more promoters (assets) and fewer detractors (liabilities) drives sustainable growth. But we knew we needed to reinforce NPS in a more objective way. Even when augmented with digital signals and big-data tracking, survey scores are inherently soft. Executives (and investors) need a hard metric to which people can be held accountable.

Reichheld had his "aha!" about earned growth while studying an investor presentation slide in preparation for a keynote at First Republic Bank's executive conference. The bank had quantified how much of its growth resulted from customers' coming back for more—and bringing their friends. The slide showed that existing customers accounted for 50% of the growth in deposit balances, and referred customers another 32%. In other words, 82% of the bank's growth in deposits came from delivering great customer experiences. In loans, 88% of growth resulted from making current customers happy.

The bank has data on referrals because it asks each new customer about the primary reason for selecting the bank and records the answer in the customer's file. The bank's customer accounting system automatically consolidates households with any related small businesses, so the bank can also easily see how much existing customers' deposits and loan balances have grown. The primary reason First Republic collects this data is to prove to investors (and regulators) that its rapid growth is safe and high quality. The bank has been growing loans 15% a year in an industry that typically grows 2% to 3% a year. In many cases that would raise a red flag, since it might suggest the bank was lowering credit standards to gain share. But the data demonstrated that it was growing without adding risk. Its new business came from customers it already knew well—and from individuals referred by long-term customers.

The presentation slide inspired Reichheld to develop a new metric, *earned growth rate,* which measures the revenue growth generated by returning customers and their referrals. A related statistic, the *earned growth ratio,* is the ratio of earned growth to total growth. That is what First Republic illustrated in its slide—82% for deposits and 88% for loans. Since the bank's total loan growth was 15% a year, its earned growth rate in loans was 13.2%. We predict that few other banks will be able to match First Republic's earned growth performance, but we won't really know for sure until more banks start measuring and reporting their own earned growth statistics. We do know that the portion of new customers generated by referral at First Republic—71%— far exceeds the portion seen at its peers in retail banking (measured through Bain's NPS Prism research), where it ranges from 21% to 53%.

Comparing the quality of two firms' growth

Companies with the same revenue growth may have starkly different earned growth rates. The hypothetical firms in this exhibit have increased revenue at a similar pace. But by looking closely at the sources of this revenue one can see that Company A has earned its growth by satisfying existing customers who come back for more and bring their friends, while Company B has generated significant revenue by aggressively buying new customers through advertising and promotions.

Company A: Growth through earning new customers

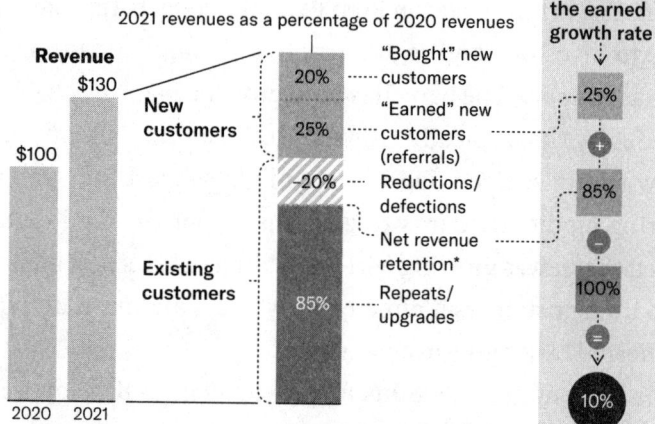

2021 revenues as a percentage of 2020 revenues

Calculating the earned growth rate

Revenue

$130

$100

2020   2021

New customers
- 20% ···· "Bought" new customers
- 25% ···· "Earned" new customers (referrals)

Existing customers
- −20% ···· Reductions/defections —— Net revenue retention*
- 85% ···· Repeats/upgrades

25%
+
85%
−
100%
=
10%

Company B: Growth through buying new customers

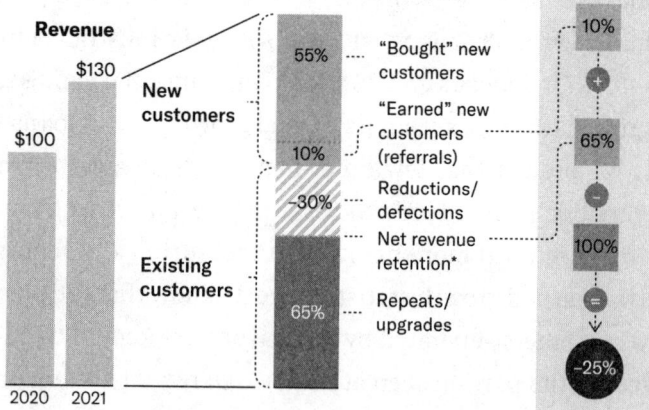

Revenue

$130

$100

2020   2021

New customers
- 55% ···· "Bought" new customers
- 10% ···· "Earned" new customers (referrals)

Existing customers
- −30% ···· Reductions/defections —— Net revenue retention*
- 65% ···· Repeats/upgrades

10%
+
65%
−
100%
=
−25%

*To calculate net revenue retention, divide current period revenues from customers who were already on the books at the beginning of the period by total revenues from the previous period.

In a very different industry, Warby Parker, the direct-to-consumer pioneer in prescription eyeglasses, earns almost 90% of its new customers through referrals. Warby was one of the first places where we tested the earned growth framework. The metric helped us appreciate Warby's impressive loyalty-based growth. The company is a longtime practitioner of NPS and plans to continue using Net Promoter Scores as a key metric for internal management. But it also plans to augment its learning with earned growth.

Calculating Earned Growth

Although it's possible to estimate earned growth without access to internal company data, investors will demand accurate (and audited) statistics based on actual results. To gather the hard data needed, firms must upgrade their systems to incorporate customer-based accounting.

Basic customer accounting continually tracks costs and revenues for each customer over time, patterns of defection, reductions, and price discounts, along with segment identifiers including tenure. It also captures the reason each customer joined (for instance, whether the customer was "earned" through referral or reputation or "bought" through advertising, promotional deals, or commission sales), along with that customer's acquisition and onboarding costs.

Essentially, this is the core information required to estimate customer lifetime value (CLV). However, CLV is complex and incorporates probabilities and higher math (think actuarial science). Although it can generate powerful insights, its application is dependent on sophisticated expertise. CLV involves a projection about the value you can expect to gain from customers, while earned growth looks at real results and quantifies the value you actually received. Earned growth can help every team learn how it is performing—by keeping track of how much growth results from customers' coming back for more and bringing their friends.

Earned growth has two elements. The first is the back-for-more component captured by a battle-tested statistic called *net revenue retention* (NRR), which is used in several industries, most notably software-as-a-service (SaaS). Once you have organized revenues by customer, you can determine your NRR. Simply tally this year's revenues from customers who were with you last year, divide that amount by last year's total revenues, and express that figure as a percentage.

The second component is *earned new customers* (ENC). It is the percentage of spending from new customers you've earned through referrals (as opposed to bought through promotional channels). This component will take a bit more effort because firms must ascertain why new customers have come on board. We have developed a practical solution to this challenge, and while it may require some experimentation and refinement, ENC is important to track. Once you have a reasonable estimate of revenues from ENC, you can better focus your customer acquisition investments—and justify more investment in delighting current customers. Firms today undervalue referrals. They treat them as icing on the cake rather than an essential (perhaps *the most* essential) ingredient for sustainable growth.

To determine your earned growth rate, begin by calculating your NRR—since this is usually the larger of the two components. To get a sense of the importance of this statistic, consider the sensitivity of SaaS companies' valuations to modest shifts in their NRR. Firms with NRR over 130% are valued more than 2.5 times higher those with NRR below 110%.

Despite its importance, even experienced SaaS firms report NRR inconsistently. Some use samples of customers, some exclude new customers who also defect within the same period or customers with multiyear contracts, and so on. Our strong recommendation to regulators is to make this a formal Generally Accepted Accounting Principles (GAAP) metric with precise reporting rules. Quantifying NRR may require homework in some industries. For example, not all brands consolidate household accounts across multiple product lines or services. Accounting for customers who join and defect within the same period must be handled consistently. Business-to-business firms will require rules for determining whether separate divisions (or purchasing units) of the same company represent one or multiple customers. But with today's sophisticated customer relationship management (CRM) technology, big-data tools, and a little analyst elbow grease, all that is doable, and it will require less work than arcane accounting metrics like goodwill and depreciation—which are demanded by GAAP but provide far less useful information.

Now let's consider how best to approach the second component of earned growth: the portion of revenues resulting from newly acquired earned customers. Few firms can quantify this today, so we have pioneered a solution that is proving effective in several ongoing beta tests. We add a relatively painless step to the process for onboarding new customers: asking them the primary reason they decided to give the company their business. By doing this right at the beginning of the relationship, we ensure that the decision is fresh in the customer's mind.

The reasons given are then sorted into earned versus bought categories. For example, if a customer chooses "trustworthy reputation" or "recommendation from friends or family," that customer and associated revenues count as earned. Customers who select "helpful salesperson," "advertisement," or "special deal or promotional pricing" are tagged as bought. Our goal is to develop a universally applicable process so that every firm can use the same methodology, resulting in comparable reported numbers. But for now a good solution is to pick the handful of reasons you expect customers will choose along with an open-ended "other" response where verbatim comments will help you adjust or augment the categories over time.

Tracking the behaviors of customers tagged as earned versus bought will help you determine their relative lifetime value, illuminating which customer segments and acquisition channels represent the best investments. In our consulting work we've seen that most firms find earned new customers to be far more profitable than bought customers, many of whom are revealed to be money losers over their life cycle. This customer-based accounting data is vital for implementing customer strategies such as those developed by our Bain colleague Rob Markey. (See "Are You Undervaluing Your Customers?" HBR, January–February 2020.) Viewing customers as a company's most important asset is just talk until each customer's value is tracked and quantified.

To determine your earned growth rate, add NRR and ENC together and then subtract 100%. Let's look at a hypothetical example. Company A's revenues grew from $100 in 2020 to $130 during 2021, or 30%. In 2021, customers who were on the books in 2020 accounted for $85 of revenues. Some of them expanded their purchases by a total of $5, but that growth was more than offset by other customers who reduced purchases by a total of $20, resulting in an NRR of 85%. New customers accounted for $45 in revenues—$25 from earned new customers (referrals) and $20 from bought new customers. Adding the NRR (85%) and ENC (25%) and then subtracting 100% results in a 10% earned growth rate.

Next, consider another hypothetical firm with the same reported revenue growth as Company A but very different sources of growth. Company B has an NRR of only 65%—far lower than Company A's. Although the two companies appear to be on the same trajectory, Company B is achieving its revenue growth by aggressively buying new customers. (See the exhibit "Comparing the quality of two firms' growth.") That will almost certainly penalize current and future earnings and prove to be an unsustainable strategy. Today's GAAP accounting obscures this vital difference.

The real-world business impact of customer loyalty hasn't been lost on savvy investors and executives. By developing auditable statistics, brands will be able to validate significant investments in providing superior customer service. Now we'll look at two actual firms, FirstService and BILT, that have begun using the earned growth rate as a gauge of customer loyalty.

The Long-Term Economic Value of Referrals

When he was just a teenager, Jay Hennick founded FirstService as a pool-cleaning company. Fifty years later, FirstService generates more than $3 billion in annual revenues and employs 24,000 people. It is North America's largest manager of residential communities, such as condominiums and homeowners' associations, and it owns a portfolio of property services, including CertaPro Painters, California Closets, Century Fire Protection, and First Onsite.

FirstService began implementing NPS across all its businesses in 2008. When Reichheld met the current CEO, Scott Patterson, in 2011, Patterson explained that he was keenly interested in finding out more about how NPS could help his business leaders build even stronger relationships with customers. The more we learned about the company, the more intrigued we became (Reichheld eventually joined its board), mostly because it seemed to care about customer loyalty as much as we do. When Patterson heard about Reichheld's plans to develop earned growth, he responded: "That's a great idea. It perfectly reflects the way we think here at FirstService."

FirstService attributes much of its success to a customer-focused culture. All its local business leaders understand the enormous expense required to replace a customer lost through defection. They also know how much more efficient it is to earn new customers through word of mouth from existing customers. Patterson estimates that more than half of all new customers in its Residential business (that is, residential-community management) are referrals. In its California Closets unit, 70% of the quality leads are. In painting, CertaPro finds that 80% to 90% are. Local franchisees know that word-of-mouth leads are likely to result in good business (CertaPro closes on more than 90% of them—about twice the rate for other leads). And because franchisees remain close to the customer, they can learn who made a recommendation and ask the recommender what turned them into a promoter.

FirstService provides a compelling example of how investors win with customer loyalty. The firm listed its stock on the NASDAQ exchange early in 1995. When a Bain team examined all U.S. public companies that had revenues of at least $100 million that year—approximately 2,800 companies—and ranked them by their total shareholder return through the end of 2019, FirstService ranked eighth (ahead of superstars such as Apple), with an annual total shareholder return of almost 22% a year. One hundred thousand dollars invested in FirstService stock in

1995 would have grown to $13.6 million by 2019. By tracking and publishing auditable earned growth rates, companies like First-Service will be able to credibly demonstrate the sources of their advantage and thereby help investors understand the sustainability of growth generated by loyalty.

Patterson admits that he struggles to convince investors of the sustainable advantage that FirstService's customer-centric culture delivers. "They hear my words," he says, "but their financial mindset just can't make sense of them. They keep asking for the real secret sauce behind our impressive track record so they can assess our future." He views the development of a measurable science around earned growth as advantageous. He's not worried about giving away the secret sauce—after all, a service-based culture is hard to build and maintain.

BILT Pioneers Earned Growth Reporting

In 2016, BILT launched a mobile app to replace paper instructions with step-by-step 3D instructions for products requiring assembly, installation, setup, repair, or maintenance. Manufacturers and retailers send BILT computer-aided design files for products, and BILT converts them into digital animations with voice instructions and text prompts.

Amazon, IKEA, and Wayfair have acknowledged the negative impact that poor assembly processes have on customer experiences, and they've tested new methods to simplify home assembly. In 2017, IKEA purchased TaskRabbit, an online marketplace that today provides access to more than 100,000 freelancers, to make it easier for its customers to hire a handy person during the checkout process. Wayfair has partnered with Handy.com to offer a similar service. Earlier this year, Amazon began experimenting with a premium service that automatically includes assembly upon delivery.

BILT helps retailers eliminate the added expenses associated with assembly and customer support calls, and it gives buyers the knowledge and coaching needed to put items together on their own. BILT even keeps track of the time that people spend on each instruction screen, which helps manufacturers and retailers identify steps in the assembly process that are confusing or non-intuitive so that they can modify and improve the experience. The app also provides consumers with a virtual filing cabinet for all product registrations, warranty information, instructions, and troubleshooting tips. Updates to instructions saved in the filing cabinet are made in real time, so they never become obsolete. In other words, BILT helps retailers and brands improve customer experiences even after a product is assembled.

At the end of the assembly process, the BILT app generates a classic NPS survey asking how likely the consumer would be to recommend the product on a scale of 0 to 10, with an open-ended question about the reason for the rating and how the experience could be improved. Because of this, the app can provide retailers with rich customer feedback linked to specific SKUs and customer purchase records.

The firm's mission, according to its website, is to create "an experience so enabling and empowering, it transforms consumers into promoters of the brands we serve." It's fascinating to see the emergence of a business entirely devoted to helping other companies improve their NPS results.

When Reichheld first encountered BILT, in early 2020, its revenues were growing more than 175% a year. As happens at most startups, the business was eating up cash. But BILT's NRR was running at 150%, and most of its new customers came through referrals—resulting in an earned growth rate of 160%. That evidence persuaded Reichheld that the company's growth was sustainable. Since then, he has made a substantial investment in BILT and joined its board of directors.

Prosper by Helping Others

We had no idea how far-reaching our impact on the customer-centricity movement would be when Reichheld began writing about loyalty in *Harvard Business Review* more than three decades ago (in "Zero Defections: Quality Comes to Services," September–October 1990). We're proud of what we've helped companies accomplish, but we realize there is still very far to go.

Early on, we saw that customer loyalty had little to do with marketing gimmicks and slick advertising, and we later proved that it generates bountiful economic advantages, including efficient customer acquisition.

Today we can establish that business success begins with leaders who embrace a fundamental proposition that their firm's primary purpose is to treat customers with loving care. That approach begets loyalty, which powers sustainable, profitable growth. It underpins the financial prosperity of great organizations and helps make them great places to work, but its effect has been notoriously difficult to quantify. It's time to get serious about measuring (and reporting) the progress made toward fulfilling that purpose and to recognize that improving the lives of the people we serve is the only way to win.

Originally published in November–December 2021. Reprint R2106E

3

Analytics for Marketers

by Fabrizio Fantini and Das Narayandas

Advanced analytics can help companies solve a host of management problems, including those related to marketing, sales, and supply-chain operations, which can lead to a sustainable competitive advantage. For example, firms can integrate decisions and optimize the entire value chain by modeling individual customers' behaviors and preferences and offering tailored products priced as close as possible to shoppers' willingness-to-pay price points—all while reducing the cost of servicing individual transactions.

But as more data becomes available and advanced analytics are further refined, managers may struggle with when, where, and how much to incorporate machines into their business analytics, and to what extent they should bring their own judgment to bear when making data-driven decisions. The questions they need to answer are: When does it make sense to shift from traditional human-centered methods to greater automation of analytics and decision-making? And how can we strike an appropriate balance between the two?

One of us (Fabrizio) founded a practice that helps clients optimize performance using AI to automate pricing and supply-chain decisions; the other (Das) is an academic who has developed an MBA course that incorporates field cases focused on using AI to enhance marketing, sales, and support functions. Together we set out to understand how to maximize the potential of both humans and machines to arrive at the best business decisions.

In general, humans are more capable in the areas of intuition and ambiguity resolution; machines are far superior at deduction, granularity, and scalability. How can you find the right balance? There are three common approaches to analytics: *descriptive*, where decisions are made mainly by humans; *predictive*, where machines determine likely outcomes, but humans choose which course to follow; and *prescriptive*, which usually means autonomous management by machines. This article describes when and how to use each approach and examines the trade-offs and limitations. (Although the focus here is on marketing and sales, the principles may be applied more broadly.)

Three Approaches to Analytics

The role of machines differs significantly in these approaches— from a tool to help managers understand a business situation, to an aid that supports managers' decisions, to a decision-maker that relieves managers of that duty. Let's explore each.

Descriptive: Aggregated observations

In descriptive analytics—commonly termed "business intelligence"—managers use machines to make sense of patterns in historical data. They essentially ask, "Help me understand what happened." That help commonly takes the form of dashboards

Idea in Brief

The Challenge

As more data becomes available and advanced analytics are further refined, managers may struggle with when to trust machines and when to trust their gut.

The Difference

Humans are better at decisions involving intuition and ambiguity resolution; machines are far superior at decisions requiring deduction, granularity, and scalability.

The Guidance

The authors' framework suggests the best approach—and balance between human and machine—given the type of decision to be made and the data available.

that highlight the input and output performance variables, enabling managers to decide which dial to turn and by how much on the basis of historically observed facts.

Descriptive analytics is about making sense of the past to inform the future. Past data is specific, clear, and certain, and this approach is rooted in verifiable and objective facts. We expect that descriptive analytics will remain part of business managers' daily experience. But because humans can't process enormous amounts of granular data, they must rely on highly aggregated information. Decisions based on that data tend to be coarse in nature, and they require the nontrivial step of extrapolating past trends and projecting them into the future.

Furthermore, descriptive analytics tends to be overly reliant on internal transaction data, which is the lowest cost, most readily available data. External data, such as customer-related data (a Net Promoter Score, for example) and market survey data, are more expensive and time-consuming to source; they are also

Three approaches to analytics

Different management problems are best solved by different analytics approaches. As decisions require less intuition and ambiguity resolution, and more deduction, granularity, and scalability, data and algorithms play a bigger role.

Approach	Descriptive: Business intelligence *What happened?*	Predictive: Prediction engines *What will happen?*	Prescriptive: Decision automation *What should I do now?*
Role of machine	Helps me understand	Supports my decision	Tells me what to do
Size of value-creation opportunity			
Examples	Strategic planning — Initial product pricing — Scenario planning — Investor reporting	Demand planning — Discount/ promotion management — CRM segmentation — Maintenance	Inventory optimization — Price optimization — Markdown optimization — Risk optimization
Rationale	Typically little data available compared with the problem — High levels of uncertainty — Simplified manual approach	Quick-win opportunities — Relatively frequent decisions and observations — Semi-automation	Larger size of improvement prize — High frequency of decisions — Full automation

difficult to analyze and synthesize in real time. Consequently, the most common types of data used in descriptive analytics are internal and industry-performance variables, which are historically observed facts. Somewhat instinctively, managers complement backward-looking data with their own experience or received wisdom, especially when using this approach for diagnostics. Therefore, a descriptive analytics approach is heavily dependent on the intuition of specific decision-makers and on their ability to overcome their biases, such as by not cherry-picking data that validates preexisting views.

In short, the descriptive analytics approach tends to lack external perspective and to be limited to high levels of aggregation. Managers provided with business-intelligence tools rely on past experience and high-level pattern recognition to project the past into the future, often relying on their gut. That can lead to repeating time-trusted approaches to solving problems rather than finding innovative new paths. Despite the subjectivity issues associated with this approach, it is still widely used because it's relatively simple and inexpensive to develop and implement. And it relies on humans for sensemaking, which puts it squarely in the comfort zone of most managers reared in the analog world.

Predictive: Limited view of the future

With predictive analytics, machines determine the likely outcome or outcomes of a particular situation for different combinations of input variables, giving managers insight to choose the course of action whose expected result best meets their objective. Predictive analytics can be used to forecast wins and losses, calculate price elasticities, predict the impact of marketing actions on specific customers, and dynamically cluster customers in market segments. These predictions allow managers to drill down and make decisions at the transactional and tactical levels as opposed to the typically high level of descriptive analytics.

The predictive analytics approach is structurally limited. It's nearly impossible to predict future demand (let alone the future itself) with much certainty. Furthermore, even predicting individual input variables can be highly complicated: Weather, competition, and supplier performance, for example, may require their own prediction models. Such models can be not only difficult to build but also problematic because the inputs and outputs often depend on one another, forcing managers to predict input and output variables concurrently.

There are also limits to the number of input variables that can be modeled and the level of granularity that can be achieved. Although multiple factors typically influence purchase decisions, common predictive techniques such as regression, clustering, and time-series forecasting usually accommodate only a small subset of variables. That is because for a model to be valid, its variables must be independent of one another—but adding more input variables creates complex interdependencies that render the model statistically unfit. In addition, to make more granular predictions, firms must collect more granular data. For example, to predict sales of a specific product, they must collect data at the SKU level rather than the category level.

Another issue in predictive analytics is the burgeoning gap between data scientists and business scientists in terms of objectives. Data scientists are focused on improving statistical rigor, while business scientists are focused on optimizing the analytics to enhance business outcomes. For data scientists, the goal of predictive analytics might be to increase the accuracy of their model, whereas for business scientists the goal is business impact. Business scientists focus on maximizing the benefits of predictive analytics by accounting for the economic impact of a false positive (when the prediction is positive but the outcome turns out to be negative) or a false negative (when the prediction is a negative outcome and the firm decides against taking any action but would have achieved a positive outcome had it pursued the opportunity). For example, in a win/loss prediction-analytics exercise, a false positive typically results in wasted sales and marketing effort, while a false negative typically results in a wasted opportunity or lost business. Focusing only on increasing accuracy might result in a model that reduces false positives (a good outcome) but also has a high degree of false negatives, which would lead to wasted opportunities and suboptimal overall performance.

In short, predictive analytics can be problematic. Relying only on machines may lead to suboptimal business decisions and a loss of profit potential. Managers can, of course, perform manual diagnostics and predictive analyses on top of descriptive data to enhance the quality of decision-making. But that sort of ad hoc effort is subject to the same kind of biases as those observed with descriptive analytics.

Prescriptive: Granular guidance

With prescriptive analytics, machines make decisions that are based on managers' defined objectives, by employing large amounts of data to rapidly analyze market conditions and learn by designing and running large numbers of low-cost experiments and what-if scenarios. Although many of their experiments might initially be suboptimal or even downright wrong, the machines can learn rapidly, getting closer to the optimal outcome targets quickly and inexpensively. They then tell the manager what needs to be done, shifting focus from inputs (such as ensuring the accuracy of decision variables) to outputs (such as optimizing the business impact of decisions), while explicitly modeling risk and economic costs.

The optimal prescriptive decision typically depends on market prediction, which drives the expected revenues, and on uncertainty, which drives the expected costs. In predictive analytics the focus would be on forecasting the number of units expected to be sold while ignoring the level of error in demand uncertainty. The prescriptive approach takes this uncertainty into account to make profit-optimizing decisions and continually adjusts as new information becomes available. For example, a retailer with low inventory on the shelves and relatively low logistics costs might respond to the possibility of a demand uptick with an aggressive inventory-replenishment strategy. However, the same retailer, in the face of high logistics costs and market uncertainty, might find a more conservative replenishment strategy to be optimal and profit-maximizing.

Well-designed prescriptive models can deliver greater financial rewards and better business performance than descriptive or predictive models can. However, they can be very expensive and complex to set up: They require dedicated software and hardware solutions and specialized human expertise to translate management strategies into mathematical, machine-friendly optimization objectives and business rules.

The human role in all this—defining the business rules and objectives—is tremendously important. Predictive analytics depends on the ability to translate business objectives, rules, and constraints into unambiguous directions to the prescriptive machine. That, in turn, enables the prescriptive model to dynamically calibrate its own recommendations toward the direction that management has specified while guaranteeing optimal outcomes and the systematic fulfillment of all rules and constraints.

When to Use Which Approach

Moving beyond descriptive analytics to more advanced and more costly approaches requires a cost/benefit assessment. Whereas costs are related to the infrastructure, expertise, and leadership required to collect and analyze data, the benefits depend on the opportunity for extra profits that can be captured through more granular and more relevant decisions.

Therefore, which approach to use in a given situation depends on two factors: the relevance of the available data and the strength of the business case. A successful balance between human and machine maximizes the contribution of each.

Data: When available data is limited and high levels of uncertainty exist, descriptive analytics is the most viable option for providing directional guidance to managers. As the frequency of decision-making increases, more granular data becomes available, and the relevance of the data to the problem increases, more autonomous prescriptive analytics approaches tend to perform best. In intermediate cases, where only limited relevant data is available, a predictive analytics approach is preferred.

Business case: The profit-improvement potential derives from the amount of inefficiency that data-driven insights can be expected to address. But inefficiency isn't a characteristic of every business problem. And when it is an issue, it may be addressable only with data that is not readily available. Therefore, not all problems are amenable to advanced approaches.

For example, machines may struggle with problems related to setting long-term strategy and innovation, for which the initial definition of the question is actually more important than the formulation of accurate answers. But when it comes to the optimization of prices, inventories, or marketing investments, analytics offers companies substantial opportunities because accurate answers will better serve their customers' needs. For business problems with long time horizons, like planning, or high levels of intrinsic noise at the granular level, like CRM segmentation, or low marginal benefit from extreme optimization, like operations maintenance, a predictive approach tends to work best.

In a cost/benefit analysis, descriptive analytics is a "low pain/low gain" approach. It is most relevant in cases where limited data is available and a high level of uncertainty surrounds the outcome. While the absolute economic impact of each decision may be very high, the resulting improvement in performance does not justify the investments needed to incorporate machine input to enhance the quality of the predictions and decisions. At the other end of the spectrum, when a lot of data is available and there is an opportunity to enhance the economic impact in each single prediction with a high level of certainty, then prescriptive analytics makes the most sense, justifying its relatively higher degree of complexity and cost with its high return on investment. Often in these situations the absolute economic impact of individual decisions is not high, but the number of decisions being made, the upside potential in each of the decisions, and the higher levels of certainty of the outcomes over time combine to make the investment in prescriptive analytics worthwhile. Predictive analytics is the best fit in the intermediate region.

In Practice: The Evolution of Price Markdowns at Event Network

Excess inventory is a common problem. It must be sold, and usually at a discount, making price markdowns a pervasive and necessary part of inventory management. The root cause is the structural impossibility, even with a theoretically perfect forecasting model, of precisely predicting sales. Given the uncertainty of factors such as weather, competitors' actions, and macroeconomic shocks, managers tend to maintain high levels of inventory to avoid losing sales and customers.

Let's look at how Event Network (EN), which operates gift and memorabilia stores throughout the United States and Canada, handled the challenge. (Disclosure: EN is a client of Fabrizio's company, Evo Pricing.) Customer traffic at its stores, which are located in museums, zoos, aquariums, and other cultural attractions, is highly seasonal and relatively unpredictable. Each EN location carries unique inventory, often customized to the location (San Francisco or New York, for instance), the theme of the attraction (plants at a botanical garden), and the time of year (sweaters in winter). The chain's high number of SKUs—more than 100,000— posed a formidable challenge to price-markdown management.

Over time EN has used all three analytics approaches. Here's how each one worked.

Approach 1: Descriptive analytics

EN managers started by using a simple method: They offered deeper discounts on products with higher inventories that resulted from disappointing sales. To decide which products to mark down and by how much, EN managers considered measures such as historical sales per week, inventory levels, and coverage ratio (the number of days that the inventory will last given the current rate of sales).

To calculate the markdown for a product with a $10 unit cost and 10,000 units on hand, they multiplied the proposed markdown (30%) by the number of units on hand (30% × 10 × 10,000). They started with the SKU with the highest coverage ratio and worked down the list of SKUs until the total available markdown budget was spent.

This approach was ultimately unsatisfactory because it relied entirely on historical internal inventory-performance data. It did not consider customer- or context-related factors that have a significant impact on consumer demand.

Approach 2: Predictive analytics

Next, the managers used regression-based techniques to discount products with the highest price elasticity (the percentage change in sales volume expected from a given percentage change in price). They calculated price elasticity by running the regression of historical sales volumes on historical prices by category by store by week. For example, a price reduction of 10% for an SKU with a price elasticity of –2 yields a volume of sales increase of 20% (a product of –10% × –2). So going from a baseline of 100 units at $10 each earning $1,000 in revenue to selling 120 units at $9 each would lead to $1,080 in revenue, representing a gain of 8% in revenue. Similar calculations can be made for metrics such as margin and inventory level. By simulating scenarios, the managers could pick their preferred strategic objective and determine the optimal markdown mix according to its expected impact. Doing so could take into account not just internal inventory data but also the customer-demand expectation and therefore the market impact of their decisions.

The optimal markdown varied according to the managers' objective rather than sales or inventory level. Although the results of their regression models were statistically significant, the EN managers found the explanatory power of the models to be relatively low (price explained just 10% to 20% of the variance in the sales of a product). That's because many other factors than price influence sales, including weather, foot traffic, and the range of products available. Adding such variables to the model would have incurred the cost of collecting the additional data in a timely manner. Moreover, more data would increase the complexity of the calculations by introducing more noise and causing unwanted interdependencies among the variables.

The EN managers went ahead with the simple one-dimension regression of volume versus price, however crude, since it yielded results superior to those obtained using the descriptive analytics approach. The resulting improved performance also built up the EN management's appetite for the use of more advanced approaches to analytics. They became open to using a different approach altogether to overcome the structural limitations of the predictive analytics approach.

Approach 3: Prescriptive analytics

The prescriptive analytics approach that the EN managers eventually used improved on the prior two approaches by accounting for the broadest range of factors affecting consumer behavior. Using multiple data sources and advanced techniques such as machine learning and automated optimization, EN could identify which products to discount at any particular time and by how much.

The managers recognized that it was virtually impossible to rely on intuition at this level of granularity and nonlinearity. Furthermore, their journey across the different analytic approaches led them to appreciate the benefits of using automation and machine learning to make sense of complexity and to build self-learning systems that improved profitability significantly over time.

. . .

When it comes to choosing an analytics approach, it is imperative to rethink the role of the manager: from the person who has all the answers to the one who asks the right questions. The framing of problems, which can then be given to machines to solve, remains squarely a human ability. But managers can wisely cede some control to machines. The primary considerations when choosing the best approach are known and clear: the relevance and availability of data, and the potential for improvement in business impact expected from investing in more sophisticated analytics.

Humans and machines excel at different tasks: humans at dealing with limited data and applying intuition in unfamiliar contexts, and machines at making decisions, however granular and sparse, that are repeated in time or space or both, and in environments flooded with rich data. Provided with too little data, in highly ambiguous situations, or in the presence of conflicting objectives that limit what can be inferred from data, machines struggle to produce relevant outcomes. But for complex problems that have abundant relevant data and whose solutions could significantly improve business performance, managers should buy or build the right machines and set the right goals for them to do what they can do so well.

Originally published in May–June 2023. Reprint R2303E

4

Personalization Done Right

by Mark Abraham and David C. Edelman

The Spotify app knows what you want to hear. It uses AI to process a vast array of your engagement data, including the songs, podcasts, and audiobooks you've listened to, when you listened to them, and what led you to them. Its library is tagged by genre, era, tempo, mood, and a long list of other characteristics. The tags allow Spotify to collate playlists based on your listening habits. The app is always learning, constantly running micro tests with user groups. Spotify attributes a large part of its success to its personalized recommendations—its user base and revenues have both increased by 1,000% in the past decade to more than 600 million users and $14 billion, respectively.

Despite investing heavily in technology that could make personalization easier, faster, and smarter, most companies struggle to achieve Spotify's degree of personalization. In a BCG survey of 5,000 global consumers designed to gauge the effectiveness of personalized recommendations, two-thirds of respondents say they have recently experienced a recommendation that was inappropriate, inaccurate, or invasive. Despite such negative experiences, more than 80% of respondents say they want and expect personalized experiences.

Business leaders aren't responding quickly enough. A BCG survey of more than 1,400 global C-suite executives found that 85% of business leaders plan to increase spending on AI in 2024. But most of that is earmarked for cost-saving initiatives rather than personalization. That is a mistake. We believe that personalization will be the most exciting and most profitable outcome of the emerging AI boom—but only for companies that make it a strategic focus.

Unfortunately, most companies lack a clear understanding of what great personalization should look like. We attempt to remedy that problem in this article. Drawing on decades of work consulting on the personalization efforts of hundreds of large companies, we have built the Personalization Index. This metric, a single score from 0 to 100, measures how well companies deliver on the promises they implicitly make to customers when they personalize an interaction.

To be clear, personalization isn't as simple as automatically plugging customer names into emails. True personalization requires creating experiences at scale, which get fine-tuned with each successive interaction and empower customers to get what they want—faster, cheaper, or more easily. Doing so requires delivering on five implicit promises that shape customers' expectations: *empower me, know me, reach me, show me,* and *delight me.* We'll describe how the components of the index are based on these promises and show businesses how to assess their own Personalization Index score.

Idea in Brief

The Problem

In a survey of more than 5,000 consumers, more than 80% say they want and expect personalized experiences. But two-thirds say they've experienced personalization that is inappropriate, inaccurate, or invasive.

The Opportunity

Companies can use AI to create and continually refine personalized experiences at scale—empowering customers to get what they want faster, cheaper, or more easily.

The Assessment

The Personalization Index allows companies to assess how well they deliver on the promises they implicitly make to customers—and discover where they need to improve.

Building the Personalization Index

To develop the index, we surveyed 200 marketers, acted as mystery shoppers to observe how companies delivered experiences across channels, and performed a financial analysis of the impact of personalization on companies' growth and shareholder returns. We developed, tested, and refined the index's rubric internally at BCG and in our work with hundreds of clients. It uses objective questions, which allows scoring to remain consistent, whether the assessment was conducted by someone at BCG or by clients themselves.

Our research uncovered a set of performance drivers for each component of the Personalization Index. Let's look at each one in turn and examine how personalization leaders—companies that score in the top quartile of the index overall and excel in at least one area—are getting it right.

Empower me

Personalization leaders start by asking: How can I make the customer's experience better by personalizing it? They understand customers' unique needs at every step of their journey and decide how personalization can best help them. This is the most important component of the Personalization Index. To determine this score, we use mystery shopping activities and customer surveys to assess the level and quality of personalization that companies are delivering.

A leader in this area is SonderMind, a mental wellness company. According to the National Institute of Mental Health, almost a quarter of adults in the United States today struggle with mental health. It can be confusing to navigate the various treatment options, so SonderMind set out to empower its users to find help more easily. SonderMind's app personalizes patient journeys on the basis of interactive experiences that assess 12 brain functions (such as mental-processing speed and a predisposition to anxiety and depression), and patients log their progress against goals they set. While protecting individual patient privacy, the app learns from the experiences of its many users and can suggest simple actions for each user to take (in addition to connecting with a therapist)—for example, practicing a meditation exercise or keeping a diary of one's feelings. It also arms therapists with tools to develop the optimal treatment plan, based on anonymized data about what has worked for similar patients. The result has been a win-win: lower costs for insurers and better outcomes for patients.

Know me

Personalization leaders win their customers' trust; they are granted permission to securely collect their data and use insights culled from it to improve the customer experience. Here, we look at the number and depth of digital relationships a company has with customers and its ability to retain them. We also look at the maturity of its customer data management and identity matching. Spotify is one of a dozen or so large brands that have an average of upward of 600 million monthly users. But personalization leaders don't have to be the largest in their categories to deliver on this promise. Sweetgreen, a newcomer to the restaurant business relative to the largest chains, illustrates this point well. Right from its start, in 2007, it invested in building digital relationships with customers. It launched a mobile app in 2013, ahead of many large restaurant chains, and progressively added features such as mobile ordering, delivery, personalized offers and challenges, and a loyalty program to drive digital engagement. Sweetgreen stands out not only in terms of its share of sales through digital channels (around 60% in 2023) but also in terms of engagement: customers who use its digital channels order more frequently, and spend more on average, than those who come in to order salads at one of its brick-and-mortar locations.

Reach me

Having the data to know the customer is not enough. Leaders use AI to identify triggers to reach out, such as when a customer browses online or makes an inquiry. Moreover, they invest in orchestrating touches across channels and use smart frequency management to ensure that their touches are coordinated, not overwhelming. To assess an organization's maturity in this area, we examine the sophistication of its targeting intelligence, how advanced its experimentation capabilities are (as measured by the volume, speed, and scale of its experiments), and how well it orchestrates actions across channels.

Although Cisco focuses primarily on B2B customer experiences, it turned to personalization to enable its account teams and customers to navigate its ever-growing range of products and services. It recognizes that every client has a different context and that clients' situations can change rapidly. So it combined a wide range of data sources across the company, including product use, service requests, marketing interactions, and even external triggers such as financial news. Coordinating all this data has made Cisco a personalization leader. Its sales team knows whom to contact, when, and about what, and comes armed with relevant content and demos. Because Cisco's sales and marketing teams are closely linked, customers get coordinated exposure to content that supports their needs and that opens up sales dialogues. Leveraging data on interactions around the world, Cisco uses AI models to understand the appropriate level of engagement for each account and to suggest the right timing to approach contacts. The models also make recommendations that marketers and salespeople can act on. Adoption of these tools quickly accelerated as salespeople found they could grow their account portfolios without losing momentum with their existing key accounts.

Show me

Personalization leaders build and manage robust content libraries that they tailor to the unique needs of each customer—while staying true to their brand voice. To do this, many are leveraging generative AI tools to create content. To evaluate companies on this promise, we looked at how sophisticated their content creation and management capabilities were and how well they personalized text, images, and videos for individual customers.

The global jewelry brand Pandora thrives by sparking customer interest with inspirational content. As part of its strategy, it uses AI-generated content to tailor its messaging to each customer and cut cycle times for certain types of content creation from 12–14 months to a mere 10 days. The company learned that personalizing the background and model image for each individual—and coordinating how the customer sees those images across emails, websites, and other ads—substantially improved conversion rates.

Delight me

Personalization leaders adopt agile ways of working to accelerate the testing and learning that improve the intelligence behind each customer interaction. As noted earlier, true personalization requires that the quality and value of customer experiences be continually fine-tuned. Our research shows that the *delight me* promise is the hardest to deliver on. It requires relentless experimentation. The more customers you test with, in ever-faster cycles, the more learning you capture and feed into your AI engines, optimizing what you can deliver at increasingly granular levels. This level of personalization requires technology, but it also requires new operating processes that marry AI with organizational intelligence. Therefore, we measure the speed and scale of the company's test-and-learn process, the sophistication and automation of its measurement, and how the organization is set up for personalization—for instance, the prevalence of cross-functional agile teams, a clear owner of the initiative, and committed funding.

Many of the personalization leaders that set the bar in this area are digital natives. DoorDash runs hundreds of micro-experiments in its app, testing things such as improvements in add-to-cart and product-substitution recommendations. It has designed its app

and its tech infrastructure to quickly run and measure such experiments, and it operates agile teams that act on the learnings to
improve each personalized digital experience.

More-traditional companies often fail a few times before they
manage to emulate these approaches. We recently worked with
a large U.S. bank that had created a team charged with breaking
down silos to deliver greater agility throughout the company.
But all it did was create yet another silo. We disbanded it and
replaced it with a cross-functional "agile" pod, made up of in-
house representatives from marketing, analytics, IT, creative,
data science, and engineering. The participants had the authority and the budget to take meaningful action. They were tasked
with a common goal of increasing the speed of testing. Within
two months they cut the bank's traditional 12-week campaign-
development process down to three days. Capitalizing on that
drastically shorter cycle time, they launched hundreds of new
tests, exponentially increasing their rate of learning. Those
actions cut the bank's credit card churn rates in half and dou-
bled the rate of converting leads into new active card members.

As those examples illustrate, getting personalization right
has many components, but a marketer who is reasonably familiar with the company's personalization capabilities can complete a reliable self-assessment with a 15-minute survey. A full
assessment can be done in a couple of weeks. We believe that it is
worth your time and effort.

The Power of Personalization

The nature of competition is changing. Instead of competing on
manufacturing scale, companies are competing on the scale of
customer interactions, by building up their loyalty programs,

app registrations, authenticated website users, and reasons to interact across the customer journey, to name a few examples. They compete on the speed at which they learn from interactions by testing variations in every interaction. They also compete on their ability to use their learning to tailor the customer experience by having cross-functional teams that constantly experiment with new experience designs, content, timing, channels, and the like. Here are several high-level takeaways from our research into personalization that can help businesses move forward.

Personalization leaders can be found in every industry

Across the 12 industry segments we reviewed, companies today score, on average, only 49 on the Personalization Index. The average score of companies in the top decile is 72. Unsurprisingly, the index leaders tend to be digital natives, such as Netflix, Uber, Alibaba, and Amazon, along with other early movers in the personalization space, such as Starbucks and Sephora. But we found leaders in almost all sectors.

We have already highlighted some in media (Spotify), health care (SonderMind), restaurants (Sweetgreen), B2B technology (Cisco), fashion (Pandora), and delivery services (DoorDash, a digital native). The differences within sectors are more pronounced than those across sectors. In addition to digital natives, the food, drug, and mass retail sectors also rate highly as a group—not surprising, given the data-rich loyalty programs, high purchase frequencies, volume of touchpoints, and number of products in those sectors, all of which enable companies to collect more data in less time. Although companies in more highly regulated industries, such as insurance, financial services, and health care, tend to score lower on the index, some firms in those sectors have leapfrogged their competitors.

Advanced personalization generates lots of revenue

Companies that put personalization and AI at the center of their customer strategy are growing 10 percentage points faster than personalization laggards and six points faster than companies on average (see the exhibit "Better personalization leads to faster growth"). The data shows that personalization leaders have more digital customer relationships, and their customers spend 30% more than customers as a whole in their category. The root cause of this difference is that their customers engage three times as often (not just by transacting but also pre- and post-purchase) as do the customers of their competitors. As a result, the leading companies generate more data and insights on which to base future personalized interactions.

Scaling personalization across customer interactions is crucial

Achieving the highest levels of customer satisfaction is possible only when a company delivers on personalization at scale—that is, in more interactions, with as many customers as possible, and while leveraging the benefits of detailed data in every interaction. When we examined the link between customer satisfaction (measured by a company's Net Promoter Score) and the Personalization Index, we observed a positive correlation. For every 10 points higher that a company scored on the index, its Net Promoter Score tended to increase by an average of seven points. The levels of customer satisfaction at companies that score low on the index vary widely. Indeed, some companies with exceptional service and value don't rely on personalization—think of a low-cost retailer known for its private-label quality or a no-frills airline known for on-time arrivals. However, the relationship

Better personalization leads to faster growth

Companies that excel at personalization grow faster than those that don't. When we compared companies that scored in the top decile on the Personalization Index with those that had an average score, we found a difference of six percentage points in their compound annual growth rate.

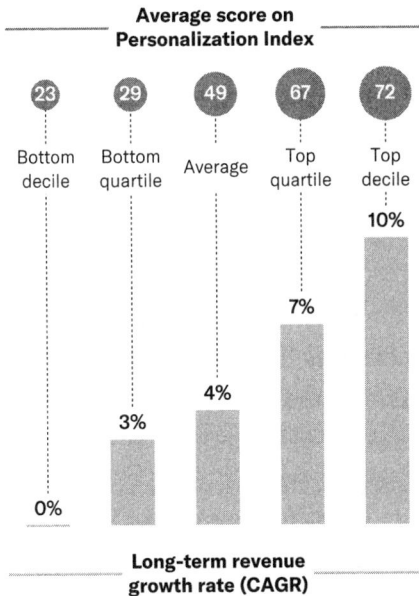

**Average score on
Personalization Index**

23	29	49	67	72
Bottom decile	Bottom quartile	Average	Top quartile	Top decile

10%

7%

4%

3%

0%

**Long-term revenue
growth rate (CAGR)**

Note: We looked at the CAGR of publicly listed companies from 2018 to 2023, where data was available and excluding companies that had made major acquisitions.

Source: BCG Personalization Index research; Mark Abraham and David C. Edelman, *Personalized: Customer Strategy in the Age of AI* (Boston: Harvard Business Review Press, 2024).

between index ranking and customer satisfaction is clearest among personalization leaders. All top-scoring companies in the Personalization Index had NPS scores above 30, and only companies with high index scores had NPS scores above 40. By building personalization programs that scale up, companies can truly stand out among the world's best and achieve the highest levels of customer satisfaction.

Personalization leaders deliver superior value creation

We examined the value creation track record of personalization leaders over time. The top quartile of companies in the Personalization Index outperformed not only the laggards but also the market index over three, five, and 10 years. The performances of the leaders and the laggards were already markedly different before 2020, but the Covid-19 pandemic accentuated the gap. One dollar invested in a personalization leader would have yielded three dollars after five years; the same investment in a personalization laggard would be worth only 50 cents.

These results show that companies that successfully execute personalization at scale are growing faster, delighting their customers, and creating superior value as they capture share from competitors. After crunching the numbers on the relative growth rates of personalization leaders and laggards by sector and taking into account the size of each sector, we estimate that a $2 trillion prize is waiting to be captured across industries by personalization leaders.

Voya Financial Keeps the Promises of Personalization

One company that's realizing the potential of personalization is Voya Financial. Recognizing that employee benefits were becoming a no-win commodity game, Voya's leaders set out to differentiate the firm. They positioned it as a partner that would improve how its clients' employees managed their finances while delivering superior economics for employers. To do that, they focused on pulling together a complete financial picture for registered users—including their retirement plans, personal financial activity, and health-care benefits. Voya examined how people make financial decisions and discovered numerous opportunities to be a better partner. If it could get a more complete picture of customer financials, executives realized, it could dramatically improve its ability to inform customers about their situations and recommend options.

Voya's leaders started by recognizing that most people don't really understand how their disparate financial relationships fit together. Their research showed that few people had thought through how their health-care costs were likely to affect their financial plans, or why their retirement and personal savings should have different goals and get different tax treatment. So they first focused on bringing together all the data, educating their members, and providing a single app, My Voyage, where members could see and add to their financial profiles.

Then Voya experimented with new customer experiences that were driven by personalization. When customers gave Voya a full picture of their financial portfolios, the company quickly produced recommendations for rebalancing the portfolios for optimal health, even if it meant money would be moved out of Voya accounts. By being objective, Voya built trust, and members felt encouraged to add more of their accounts outside Voya into the app.

Next Voya built a "test engine" to relentlessly experiment in order to learn how best to encourage members to take a useful action, such as increasing their retirement contributions, setting up a health savings account, or moving personal savings into an account with better interest rates. The company started with its own employees, working through the execution issues and building its base of data. Then it scaled up those efforts and continually learned from its experiments. AI capabilities helped spot which members would benefit, helped set up the cells for testing multiple variables, and generated creative variants for the program team to consider.

Taken together, these personalization efforts contributed to not only a growth in accounts and double-digit revenue growth but also widespread accolades. Voya was named one of the "Most Trusted Financial Services" brands by *Newsweek* in 2023 and one of the "World's Most Ethical Companies" by Ethisphere.

Calculating Your Index Score

Now that we've proved the power of personalization, we'll help you determine your company's index score.

Empower me (50 points). Begin by assessing the actual level of personalization you deliver to your customers in each step of their journey across all your channels. Because delivering on the first promise of personalization, *empower me,* is the most important, this score makes up half the Personalization Index score. To determine your score, identify the steps of your customer's journey and the channels where personalization truly matters and can make the experience better, faster, or more convenient. (That will depend on the categories you play in, your customers' expectations, and how well your competitors are personalizing.) Then look at what real customers recently experienced and evaluate whether you are personalizing "fully 1:1," "extensively," "moderately," or "not at all," and assign yourself points accordingly.

Next take an honest look at your organization's capabilities in delivering personalization at scale.

Know me (10 points). Measure the number and quality of the digital customer relationships you have relative to the total customer base in the markets you serve. Ask yourself how easily you can contact these customers across channels and how advanced your data management practices are. For example, how do you handle data governance? And have you built a customer-360 database leveraging universal customer-identity matching?

Reach me (10 points). Measure how finely tuned your targeting models are. Are you using automated experimentation and machine learning to optimize the next best action for your customers and orchestrating across channels? Leaders leverage machine-learning AI solutions while laggards pull customer-targeting lists manually, with limited segmentation.

Show me (10 points). The length of time it takes you to launch a personalized campaign is a good barometer of your company's maturity on this dimension. (Laggard organizations take 12 or more weeks, but leaders take a few days.) It is also worth assessing how advanced your automated content creation and management capabilities are. Leaders leverage well-tagged content libraries and the latest gen AI solutions, paired with automated content creation processes, whereas laggards manually create each campaign, with little reuse of assets.

Delight me (10 points). Measure how well and how quickly you can test, learn from, and improve the customer experience. Diagnose whether you have organizational or technological impediments to measuring progress on personalization and implementing improvements on a weekly or more frequent basis.

Sample Personalization Self-Assessment

To complete a self-assessment, companies must answer dozens of questions related to their personalization efforts. The following is a small sample of questions marketers should ask to determine the maturity of their personalization efforts. You can take the Personalization Index survey at on.bcg.com/personalization.

Empower Me

- Do we personalize experiences at each step of engagement throughout the customer journey?
- Do we provide cross-channel personalization capabilities?
- Is every communication channel used for personalization?

Know Me

- Does customer data live in a single repository?
- Is customer data integrated throughout our other marketing systems?
- Do we have high-quality identity resolution in place?

Leaders learn 10 times as fast as laggards do; they run hundreds of experiments and turn around improvements in days, while laggards take many months to achieve the same feat.

And finally, be accountable (10 points). After you've assessed your performance on the five implicit promises, ask yourself whether your organization has a senior leader who is accountable for personalization, with P&L responsibility and a cross-functional mandate. In the large companies we studied, we have

Reach Me

- Do we conduct A/B testing on our personalization efforts?
- Have we deployed a next-best-action decisioning or product recommendation engine?
- Do we automate customer segmentation?

Show Me

- Do we offer tailored experiences on a 1:1 basis for every customer? 10:1? 100:1?
- Are we able to conduct personalized experiences or campaigns quickly from ideation to launch?
- Do we use gen AI to automate the production of marketing collateral?

Delight Me

- Do organizational or technological impediments keep us from measuring progress on personalization?
- Do we run weekly tests related to personalization?
- Do we implement improvements on a weekly or more frequent basis?

often found this to be what makes the difference between success and failure in personalization. That's why having such a senior leader in place is worth the final 10 points on the index.

Lessons from the Leaders

Personalization leaders follow a playbook to deliver on each of the five promises of personalization, starting with how to empower the customer. Senior executives looking to accelerate their own personalization efforts can follow that playbook no matter how mature their current personalization efforts are. We have found three areas of focus that make the difference between success and failure.

Rethink leadership roles and set a clear vision

Because personalization is such a cross-functional effort, its mandate must come from the CEO, and the C-suite should rally around a shared strategic vision. Every C-suite executive should explicitly support the vision and be accountable for delivering on it. The CFO, for instance, must understand the business case. The CDO (chief digital officer) needs to be accountable for the digital experience. The CMO must instill agile marketing practices. The chief data and analytics officer (CDAO) needs to build robust platforms and intelligence. The COO needs to rethink the processes required to deliver a personalized customer experience, and the general counsel must champion responsible personalization and AI principles in partnership with the CDAO. The CIO needs to prioritize and deliver on the right technology investments in constant partnership with the business, and so on. Ultimately, as we explained in "Customer Experience in the Age of AI" (HBR, March–April 2022), small agile teams comprising many of these functions need to deliver on each wave of personalization use cases.

Secure the personalization foundation

The Personalization Index, paired with your strategic plan, will quickly highlight the gaps in your foundational capabilities. The key to success is prioritizing how to address those gaps and tying the upside and investments associated with each to the overall business case. Personalization leaders also apply the principles of smart integration. (For more detail, see

"What Smart Companies Know About Integrating AI," HBR, July–August 2023.) They recognize that not everything has to be built internally, and the integration of the parts is just as important as the selection of the right components. In our experience, personalization can be largely self-funding, even in the initial years, when the right trade-offs are made. As the teams deliver concrete business value, larger investments can be funded and the partnership between finance and a personalization team becomes even more important to ensure that a portion of the gains are regularly invested back into personalization efforts.

Compete on speed

Ultimately, personalization depends on the speed and scale of learning. Hence every organization should ask itself how teams could rethink processes to learn 10 times as fast. Many organizations are still working in eight- to 12-week campaign cycles. Three to five days is possible in every industry. Even companies that have cut their cycles down to days have a hard time taking the learnings forward quickly and enhancing the next customer interaction. Automation of specific areas (enhancing content, for example, or adjusting targeting and data science) can give teams rapid optimization tactics to improve key performance indicators (KPIs) meaningfully every week. On an annual basis, measuring how far you have progressed on the Personalization Index is a great way to hold the organization accountable.

. . .

For several decades companies have been gradually improving their financial performance by tapping the range of capabilities that can power personalization. We are now at a tipping point: Brand-differentiating personalization is not only possible but will be essential for competitive success. With the availability of new AI tools, a company's ability to embed personalization capabilities in its operations has increased dramatically.

As the Personalization Index shows, there is a marked difference between the leaders—who are reshaping their value propositions and go-to-market approaches through personalization—and those who are just using basic tech tools to bombard prospects with impersonal messages. Tomorrow's winners are already using AI to unlock personalization's potential, and they are building new sustainable advantages along the way. The time for delivering growth with AI-enabled personalization is now.

Originally published in November–December 2024. Reprint R2406G

5

What Psychological Targeting Can Do

by Sandra Matz

P sychological targeting, the practice of influencing behavior through interventions customized to personality traits, burst onto the world stage in 2018, when Cambridge Analytica's involvement in the 2016 U.S. presidential election made international headlines. The company had allegedly created psychological profiles of millions of Facebook users without their knowledge and then hit them with fearmongering political ads tailored to their psychological vulnerabilities.

Since then, there has been a lot of speculation about what psychological targeting can and cannot do. Some have declared it the next frontier of psychological warfare, while others have brushed it off as marketing swamp water.

I was one of the first scientists to study this practice and helped break the Cambridge Analytica story. Over the past 10 years I've examined how we can turn people's digital footprints—their social media profiles, search queries, spending records, browsing histories, blog posts, and smartphone data, including GPS records—into intimate predictions about their inner lives using machine learning. I've explored how such insights can be used to sway opinions and change behavior. And I've suggested ways we can implement psychological targeting ethically.

Cambridge Analytica folded amid the controversy over its data-collection and persuasion tactics, but psychological targeting as a service is very much alive and thriving. I know because I regularly get consulting requests from companies that want to implement psychological targeting and from startups trying to enter the space. They come to me with slightly different narratives, but typically their goals are similar: to create value for businesses and their stakeholders by tapping into people's psychological needs and motivations.

In this article I'll clarify what psychological targeting is actually capable of and then offer guidance on how to use it in a way that both upholds basic ethical principles and maximizes the benefits that companies and their customers realize.

What Exactly Is Psychological Targeting?

Let's start by debunking a persistent myth: Psychological targeting *isn't* the brainwashing machine Cambridge Analytica made it out to be. Even with the most accurate understanding of a person's psychological profile, you are unlikely to turn a sworn Hillary Clinton voter into a Donald Trump supporter or convert an iOS fanatic into an Android lover. But that doesn't mean it has no influence on people, either. My research (and that of others in the field) all points in the same direction: Psychological targeting is an effective marketing tool. It can be used to shift opinions and attitudes, create demand that wasn't

Idea in Brief

The Opportunity

Psychological targeting—the practice of influencing people's behavior through interventions aimed at personality traits—has come of age as a marketing tool, thanks to an explosion in data that provides insight into consumers' psyches.

The Peril

While psychological targeting can increase sales by helping a firm communicate with customers in a way that resonates, there is also the risk of backlash if they feel they're being manipulated or if data is harvested without their consent.

The Right Way

Leading marketers will put ethics front and center, using psychological targeting only when more prosaic approaches are insufficient, ensuring that they're offering greater value to the customers they target and being transparent about what they're doing and why.

there initially, and engage with consumers on a much more personal level than ever before.

Psychological targeting is qualitatively different from the psychographic targeting that was hyped in the late 1970s but failed to deliver on its promise. Traditional psychographic targeting built on the intuition of marketing professionals to define personas representing segments of customers that were based on consumers' opinions, attitudes, and lifestyle choices. In contrast, psychological targeting builds on validated psychological constructs that capture fundamental differences in how people think, feel, and behave. The most popular of such constructs is the Big Five model of personality, also known as the OCEAN model for the dimensions it measures: openness to experience, conscientiousness, extroversion, agreeableness, and neuroticism. Although there are many other dimensions that could prove valuable for psychological targeting (say, people's personal values, motivational orientation, or moral foundations), the Big Five model dominates both research and practice.

The Big Five are a valuable starting point because they can predict people's preferences for products and brands. A project my colleagues and I worked on demonstrates how. In 2016 we teamed up with a large international bank in the United Kingdom to study the spending habits of some of its customers. We had access to their self-reported personality profiles and information on every transaction they had made over the previous six months. As expected, we found that spending was clustered by personality dimension. Extroverts, for example, were more likely to spend money in restaurants and bars, while introverts were more likely to buy home appliances and books. Conscientious people invested their money in savings and children's clothes, while their more disorganized counterparts spent it on takeout and mobile phones. Not only that, but customers whose spending patterns were more aligned with those typical of their personality profiles reported more satisfaction with their lives.

Personality types predict people's preferences for marketing messages and communication styles too. Conscientious individuals, for example, love numbers and details, while less conscientious people might be more easily swayed by compelling stories. While you might impress open-minded people with eye-catching visuals and flowery language, you'd probably be better off sticking to conservative graphics and basic, respectful language with more-conventional individuals.

The large-scale application of psychological targeting was made possible by the explosion in cheap and accessible consumer data. Consider that in just one minute, Amazon customers spend

$283,000, Facebook receives 44 million views, YouTube streams 694,000 hours of video content, Instagram users share 65,000 photos, and Venmo facilitates transactions worth $304,000, according to Domo.com. While many businesses were quick to find ways to use such data to predict consumer behavior and preferences ("People who bought product X also bought product Y"), their ability to truly *understand* consumers' needs and motivations remained rather limited. For example, they didn't understand *why* customers who bought product X also bought product Y, or what might motivate them to buy product Z.

Psychological targeting promises to change that by allowing companies to translate behavioral data into personality profiles for individual customers. What might that look like in practice? One of my first industry partners was Hilton Hotels & Resorts, which wanted to use psychological targeting to create richer and more-personalized customer journeys. Working as paid consultants, my research team designed an application that allowed users to connect their Facebook profiles to one of our predictive algorithms and receive a personality-based traveler profile with customized vacation recommendations. For instance, if our algorithm suggested that a customer was introverted, that person would get a "soloist" profile with recommendations for quiet and relaxing destinations. If the algorithm indicated that someone was neurotic, we'd offer an "all-inclusive" traveler package with recommendations for worry-free vacations with nothing left to chance. The campaign, which reached 60,000 users in three months, was a success. Hilton won an award for the most innovative travel marketing campaign from the Chartered Institute of Marketing, and higher click-through and social-engagement rates meant a higher return on investment and brand visibility for the company.

In another study we teamed up with a beauty retailer to optimize its Facebook ad campaigns and increase purchases in its
online store. Though Facebook doesn't allow marketers to target
personality traits directly, its interest-based targeting option lets
them do so indirectly. If liking manga is linked to introversion,
then targeting people who follow manga on Facebook effectively
enables you to target introverts (and perhaps a few misunderstood extroverts). We decided to tailor messages to women's
psychological needs and motivations. One set of ads spoke to
extroverts' craving for stimulation, excitement, and attention,
and another set played into introverts' desire for quiet, high-
quality "me time." The extroverted ads were colorful, featuring
women in highly social settings (say, in the middle of the dance
floor) and alluding to their need to be seen ("Dance like no one's
watching, but they totally are"). The introverted ads were subtle,
showing a single woman in a peaceful context (using a cosmetic
face mask to relax) and hinting at her reserved nature in the copy
("Beauty doesn't have to shout"). The ads that were customized
by personality were 50% more effective at attracting purchases
and generating revenue than those that were not.

How to Get It Right

Over the years my team and I have tried many variations of psychological targeting, experiencing both successes and failures
and learning from both. Here's our advice for launching a psychological targeting program.

Ask, Do we really need psychological targeting?

It's possible you'd be better off using other approaches. If you simply want to predict what a customer is going to buy, for instance,

you don't need to know their psychological profile. In fact, incorporating it into your predictions could reduce their accuracy by adding noise in two areas: the translation of digital footprints into psychological insights (no model is perfect), and the translation of those insights into purchase intentions. If you take the simpler approach of trying to link past behavior to future preferences (people who buy X also buy Y), there's only one place to make mistakes.

However, there are two situations in which a psychological understanding of people is invaluable. The first is when a company sells to new customers. In that situation it essentially has no information about the customers. It can't rely on past behavior to predict future preferences. We call this the "cold-start problem." The beauty of psychological traits is that they're independent of the context they're assessed in. It doesn't matter if a company predicts a customer's extroversion level from Facebook or Twitter posts, credit-card spending patterns, purchase history, or GPS records. Putting aside measurement errors, the customer's personality assessment, from which purchasing preferences can be inferred, should always be roughly the same. An online retailer, for example, could ask new customers to log in with Facebook, use their likes and statuses to predict which ones are extroverts, and recommend products that appeal to extroverts to them. Over time, as it collects more and more purchasing data, it could phase out the personality insights and shift toward purely behavioral predictions.

The second scenario is the design of personalized marketing materials. After all, marketing is as much about *how* we communicate the value of a product as it is about the product itself. The more marketers can understand *why* someone might be interested in a particular product, the better they can tailor their creative content to those interests. Imagine you're selling flowers. Understanding whether someone might be interested in buying a bouquet as a surprise gift for someone else (a sign of agreeableness), to feel calmer and more relaxed at home (introversion and neuroticism), or to add an aesthetically pleasing touch to an office space (openness) allows you to customize your messaging appropriately.

Create a holistic customer experience

It's true that digital technology allows you to collect more consumer data than ever before. But it's also true that personalizing the customer experience is often far easier in person. A deft frontline employee can be given all sorts of discretion when it comes to meeting customer needs. Consider the hotel concierge who overhears a guest raving about a local bakery and then surprises that person with a box of pastries in her room. Most people are reasonably good at inferring the psychological traits of people they barely know and at integrating those insights into their interactions with them.

Both online personalization and offline personalization are valuable, but they often feel disconnected. Take department stores. These retailers collect behavioral customer data in order to make recommendations and send out personalized offers. Once you step into one of their locations, a retail associate will try to read your personality and mood and serve you accordingly. But the two touchpoints aren't integrated: The associate and the email marketers never talk to each other.

Psychological targeting could join the two worlds. By providing consumer insights that can be understood by both algorithms and humans, it offers a consistent "concierge service" across all channels. Regardless of whether you connect with a customer through your online store or a staff member, the customer can always be treated the same way. A department store's algorithm, for example, could figure out if a customer is extroverted or neurotic and adjust both recommendations and the content of promotional emails in response. It could also pass on that knowledge to the brick-and-mortar staff to improve the same customer's in-person experience (advising, "Don't make small talk with this customer; she's an introvert" or "Don't overwhelm the customer with options, and remind him of the return policy; he is neurotic").

Eventually, technology may even be able to decipher consumers' needs and automatically create experiences to suit them. Over time a computer experimenting with thousands of ad variants or in-store experiences might well develop a higher level of "human intuition" than any real person could. AI is already astonishingly advanced. Consider the ad copy produced by GPT-3, an OpenAI algorithm, when I recently asked it to write an iPhone ad that appeals to an extrovert: "Looking for a phone that will keep you connected to your friends and always entertained? Look no further than the iPhone! With its built-in social media apps and endless games and streaming options, you'll never be bored again."

Help your customers discover new offerings

Customers often face exploitation versus exploration trade-offs in their purchasing decisions. Should they go with the option that they know and love ("exploitation") or choose something unknown that promises to be even more amazing ("exploration")? Same haircut or new look? Favorite rooftop bar or new speakeasy? Tried-and-true seaside vacation or new adventure?

Personalized marketing is typically focused on helping consumers exploit, serving up more of the things they already know and love. If you've searched online for a Sony Alpha DSLR camera, predictive algorithms will try to sell you not only that camera but also all the related equipment and accessories. This approach can help customers find what they need in the vast sea of internet content. And often all consumers want is to find what they're looking for in a convenient way.

But focusing exclusively on exploitation can be limiting. Customers will sometimes prefer recommendations for products that are outside their comfort zone and allow them to try something new. Psychological targeting lets companies offer them. Instead of taking the search for the Sony Alpha DSLR camera as a direct targeting input, for example, an algorithm might interpret it as a sign of openness to experience and suggest a range of novel products that are still relevant. Instead of a set of spare batteries or a tripod, how about acrylic paint or a book on philosophy?

Put ethics front and center

The bankruptcy of Cambridge Analytica—which took a "Trojan horse" approach, accessing the Facebook profiles of millions of unwitting users through their friends' accounts and building psychological profiles without their knowledge—is a cautionary tale for companies that might engage in psychological targeting without consent. But using it ethically is not just the right thing to do and a way to avoid backlash. With changing regulatory landscapes and major players such as Apple restricting access to third-party data, it might soon also be the most promising business model and the only way to get at consumer data.

As scientists, my colleagues and I are expected to follow basic ethical principles in our research. The same principles should be foundational for corporate practitioners too.

Respect for people: Protect and uphold the autonomy of consumers and treat them with courtesy.

Beneficence: Abide by the philosophy of "Do no harm" while maximizing the benefits to consumers and society and minimizing the risks to all.

Justice: Follow reasonable and nonexploitative procedures that are administered fairly (for instance, that ensure all customers benefit equally).

These principles are broad enough to allow companies to adapt them to their own day-to-day business dealings. Now let's look at how they can be translated into guidelines for action, using our project with Hilton as an example.

Keep your consumers in the loop

Hilton involved its customers at every step of the way. They were told—in plain language—exactly what data would be gathered from their Facebook profiles (for example, their likes) and, more important, how it would be used. Hilton also told them what predictions it would make based on that data and assured them that no data would ever be passed on to third parties. This kind of transparency should be standard practice. Taking it a step further, companies could also give their customers the chance to interact with and revise their personality profiles. Why? First, it creates trust that will promote engagement and long-term loyalty. But equally important, predictions are never perfect. When you turn the profiling process into a two-way conversation, you can have customers correct your mistakes—an easy way to boost the quality of your insights. Taken to the extreme, this could mean replacing the automated gathering of details on psychological traits with engaging questionnaires. Instead of making educated guesses, why not ask consumers how they like to think of themselves? Or maybe who they'd like to become with the help of your products and services? This approach typically isn't possible with potential customers, but it certainly can work with existing ones.

Make personalization a key part of your value proposition

If you ask people for their data, give them back as much value and insight as possible. The goal of the Hilton traveler app was to generate more customer engagement and thus more profits. But the product offered customers suggestions for genuinely more enjoyable and appealing stays, as well as interesting insights into their travel preferences. The goal should not be for your personalization efforts to go unnoticed—but rather for them to be recognized and appreciated by customers. This will be much easier to achieve if you abandon opt-out processes and switch to opt-in mechanisms that make privacy the default and require you to spell out the benefits consumers will get by sharing their data with you.

Collect only essential data

Think of data as radioactive. Gather as little as needed and hold it only as long as needed. Hilton agreed from the very beginning that it would receive only the personality profiles of users and not the raw data that was extracted from Facebook with their consent. That data was handled by an application my lab had designed and was deleted immediately after it was no longer needed. Today many new technologies (for example, one called federated learning) can help a company get the insights it needs without collecting the actual data that produces them.

Do a gut check

Before we launched the Hilton traveler app, we held numerous focus groups with existing customers to gauge their reaction to it. But even if you can't organize such groups, you can still ask yourself how you'd feel if your loved ones (your kids, partner, or closest friends) used the product or service you're designing and shared their personal data to get it. If that thought makes you uncomfortable, something is off, and you should go back to the drawing board. Or you could take Warren Buffett's front-page test: If your hometown paper were to write about your use of psychological targeting on its front page tomorrow, and your family, friends, and neighbors read the story, how would you react?

Don't focus solely on selling

Our research team has demonstrated that psychological targeting can do more than help sell consumer products—it can be a powerful "nudging" tool to help people improve their lives. For example, in partnership with SaverLife—a U.S. nonprofit organization that has created a platform to help low-income people develop long-term saving habits—we identified each user's most salient OCEAN personality trait and then tailored the messages we sent users about a challenge (such as "Save $100 over the course of four weeks"). Those with caring personalities (that is, high agreeableness) received messages such as "Save to build a better future for your loved ones!" Competitive personalities (low agreeableness) were given prompts such as "Every penny saved puts you one step ahead of the game!" In the control condition, which used SaverLife's best-performing messaging to date, 7.4% of users managed to hit their goal. In the psychologically tailored condition, that number rose to 11.5%, a 55% increase.

Firms could even pair profit-generating and socially responsible endeavors. For instance, Hilton could use psychological profiles to nudge consumers to reduce water use or participate in local activities designed to boost ecotourism. Or a consumer-goods company could launch psychologically targeted campaigns to get people to recycle its packaging.

What is common to all these guidelines is that they don't stop at asking, What is legal? Instead they ask, What is ethical? What is the right thing to do? You might not always be able to live up to your high standards, but if you don't set them high in the first place, you certainly won't.

. . .

When I first began studying psychological targeting, a decade ago, the only way to implement it was to do all the data wrangling and analysis yourself. You had to collect a dataset combining digital footprints with self-reported personality scores, train and validate your own predictive models, and—in most cases—conduct your own research into how to talk to customers of a certain personality profile most effectively. Today you don't have to do any of that. More and more services will do it all for you—or at least a substantial part of it. For most companies, partnering with an external vendor will make sense. But it's important to be a savvy buyer—to understand what psychological targeting offers beyond traditional marketing tools, what it can and cannot do and, above all, how to use it ethically in a way that doesn't alienate your customers.

Originally published in March–April 2023. Reprint R2302K

6

Why CMOs Never Last

by Kimberly A. Whitler and
Neil A. Morgan

I n 2012 a leading retailer began looking for a new chief marketing officer. The job description made the opening sound exciting: The new CMO would play a big, important role, leading the company's efforts to boost revenues and profits. It seemed like the kind of opportunity any would-be CMO might desire.

Sure enough, the company landed a seasoned, talented executive from the consumer-packaged-goods industry, who came on board determined to make his mark.

But a year later the new CMO was feeling deeply frustrated. Given the job description, his experience, and his conversations with the recruiter and the chain's CEO, he'd assumed he'd have the authority to create a strategy for driving growth. To his surprise, his role was limited mostly to marketing communications, including advertising and social media. He had no responsibility for (and limited influence over) product launches, pricing, and store openings. The problem, he told us, wasn't that his skills prevented him from meeting the company's goals; it was that the job was so poorly designed—and there was such a mismatch between the CMO's authority and the CEO's expectations—that it would be difficult for anyone to succeed in it. Soon after he spoke with us, the CMO left the company.

In our research into what makes CMOs effective, we've heard stories like this more often than we should. To us, they're evidence that something is going very wrong in the relationship between CEOs and CMOs. A 2012 global survey by the Fournaise Marketing Group highlights the tensions between them: The results reveal that 80% of CEOs don't trust or are unimpressed with their CMOs. (In comparison, just 10% of the same CEOs feel that way about their CFOs and CIOs.) CMOs also sense a serious problem. In our own surveys, 74% of them say they believe their jobs don't allow them to maximize their impact on the business.

This troubled relationship helps explain why CMOs have the highest turnover in the C-suite. According to an analysis by Korn Ferry, they stay in office 4.1 years on average, while CEOs average 8 years; CFOs, 5.1 years; CHROs (chief human resources officers), 5 years; and CIOs, 4.3 years. Our own research indicates that churn rates may be even worse: We found that 57% of CMOs have been in their position three years or less.

But unlike CFOs, CHROs, and CIOs, whose roles are primarily inward facing, CMOs have a direct effect on the way customers engage with the firm. When new CMOs enter companies, they often change the strategic direction—which means creating new positioning, product packaging, and ad campaigns, usually at considerable expense. If job dissatisfaction or underperformance leads to a revolving door in the CMO's office, companies can experience internal disruptions, not to mention major recruiting and severance costs.

Idea in Brief

The Problem

Four-fifths of CEOs are dissatisfied with their firms' chief marketing officers. Not surprisingly, CMOs have the highest turnover in the C-suite.

Why It Happens

Most CMO jobs are poorly designed. The expectations set for the role don't align with the responsibilities given or the metrics for success.

The Solution

CEOs must decide which type of CMO they need: a strategist, who makes decisions about the firm's positioning and products; a commercializer, who drives sales through marketing communications; or an enterprise-wide leader with P&L responsibility, who does both. Recruiters should guide them through this choice and help design the job appropriately, and CMO candidates must ensure they understand the role before signing on.

Years on the job

Most chief marketing officers have not been in their positions long. More than 40% have been in their roles two years or less, and 57% have been in them three years or less.

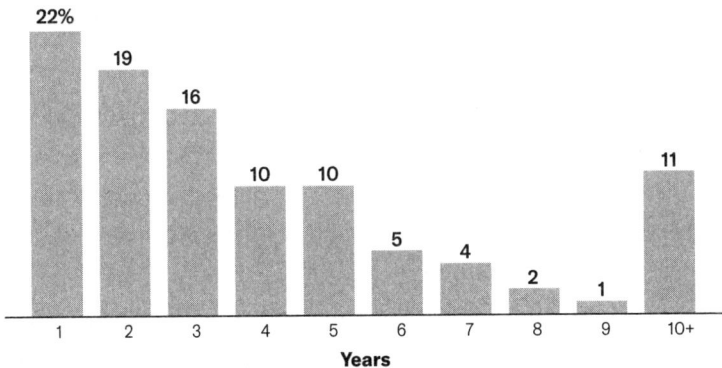

Years	Percentage
1	22%
2	19
3	16
4	10
5	10
6	5
7	4
8	2
9	1
10+	11

Source: "CMO Impact Study," 2014 and 2015, by Kimberly A. Whitler.

We believe that a great deal of CMO turnover stems from poor job design. Any company can make a bad hire, but when responsibilities, expectations, and performance measures are not aligned and realistic, it sets a CMO up to fail. In this article we'll outline the four steps CEOs should take to end this dysfunctional pattern. We'll also describe how to match the right person to the CMO job and how CEOs, executive recruiters, and CMO candidates can all work together to maximize the odds of CMO success.

Step 1: Define the Role

Let's start with a simple question: What does a CMO actually do? Surprisingly, there is no clear, widely accepted answer.

In our research we've interviewed more than 300 executive recruiters, CEOs, and CMOs; conducted multiple CMO surveys; performed an analysis of 170 CMO job descriptions at large firms; and reviewed over 500 LinkedIn profiles of CMOs. We've discovered extreme variations in the responsibilities CMOs are given and in the skills, training, and experience of the people who occupy the role. (Note that we use the term "CMO" generically to refer to a company's top marketing executive; at some firms the job may have a different title, such as executive vice president of marketing.)

Most CMOs, we've observed, have a few areas of core responsibility. More than 90% are responsible for marketing strategy and implementation, and more than 80% control brand strategy and customer metrics. But beyond that, the range of duties—from pricing to sales management, public relations to e-commerce, product development to distribution—is mind-boggling.

Three types of CMO roles

CMO jobs are not all alike. Some focus on strategy, some on commercialization, and some on both. CEOs need to understand which kind of executive their firm needs and make hires accordingly.

Enterprise-wide P&L role
Delivers profitable growth
by designing strategy and
overseeing commercialization.
Responsible for innovation,
product design, sales,
distribution, pricing, and
marketing communications.

Commercialization role
Spurs sales through
marketing communications.
Responsible for advertising,
digital content, social media,
promotions, and events.

23%

46%

Strategy role
Designs growth strategy.
Responsible for innovation,
customer insight and analysis,
and product design.

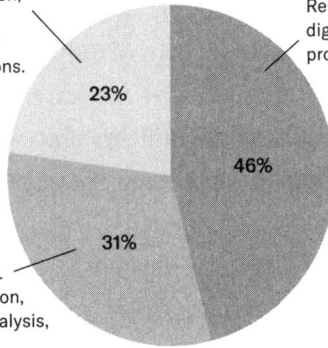

31%

Of course, not all CMO positions should be the same. Companies have different needs, challenges, and goals, and the CMO's role has to reflect those realities. Before even considering candidates for the job, a CEO must decide which kind of CMO would be best for the company. In our research we've identified three distinct types.

Some CMOs focus on *strategy*. They take the lead on up-front decisions about the firm's positioning and then translate those decisions into the design of new products, services, and experiences. Often they manage the customer insight and analytics functions. In essence, strategy-focused CMOs spearhead a company's innovation efforts. Accounting for 31% of CMOs in our research, they're common in multibrand firms and in some B2B service firms where a centralized marketing group helps set firm-level strategy.

Most CMOs focus on *commercialization*. They have a downstream role and work primarily on using marketing communications to sell the products, services, and experiences that others design. Typically, their responsibilities include overseeing traditional and digital efforts to create revenue-growing relationships with consumers. Nearly half of CMOs (46%) have this kind of role. Common in firms where a function other than marketing is central to success, commercializers play a supporting role to the function that drives innovation (such as engineers in tech firms).

The third kind of CMO handles both strategy and commercialization responsibilities in an *enterprise-wide* role focused on the design and implementation of strategy. Significantly, such CMOs have P&L responsibility and the broadest range of duties, including innovation, sales, distribution, and pricing. In our research 23% of CMOs have an enterprise-wide role. They tend to be common in single-brand firms and some consumer-packaged-goods companies. Because of the scope of their responsibilities and the organization-wide nature of their impact, marketers with this kind of experience have historically been seen as strong general managers and are often tapped for CEO roles at other firms.

How can CEOs determine which type of CMO is appropriate for their firms? They should take into account the following three external factors:

1. *The degree to which consumer insight needs to drive firm strategy.* When generating consumer insight is a critical

competency of the firm and determines the design of products, services, and experiences, the CMO role should skew toward a strategic or enterprise-wide focus. There's so much variation within industries that it's difficult to say definitively which kinds of companies fall into this category. But marketing's role should lean toward commercialization if finance, technology, manufacturing, or another inward-facing function leads a firm's strategy. This is often the situation in heavy manufacturing, industrials, technology, higher education, health care, and B2B firms. In general, when firms believe that their innovations create the need, they are less likely to look to CMOs to set strategy or boost profits.

2. *How difficult it is to achieve firm-level growth.* Companies in slow-growing or highly competitive industries are more likely to require a strategy-focused or enterprise-wide type of CMO, who can devise plans for building demand. However, if growth is easier to come by and less of a challenge for the firm, then the commercialization role may be a better fit.

3. *The level of dynamic change in the marketplace.* When a company's business model is shifting or industry boundaries are being redrawn, CMOs with strategic or enterprise-wide responsibilities are likely to be more effective. With their broader knowledge of the environment (consumers, competitors, channel partners, the marketplace) and of their firms' internal workings (core competencies, strategic direction), they can better help their management teams steer through uncertainty and rethink ways to generate demand.

It's also imperative for the CEO to consider this set of internal factors:

1. *The historical role of the CMO within the firm.* If the company's top marketing executive has traditionally focused on commercialization, shifting to a strategic or enterprise-wide role will require taking responsibilities away from another function. This becomes problematic if the other function has been managing those areas for a long time and doing it well. While it's often easier to narrow the CMO's scope, there are many times when broadening it makes sense. For instance, one CMO in higher education had a commercialization role but was elevated to a strategy role after he identified a solution to his school's admissions (and thus its growth) challenges. Expanding the CMO's responsibilities requires significant CEO involvement to communicate expectations and prevent internal backlash, however.

2. *The structure of the firm.* If a firm has multiple business units or brands, functional leadership responsibility tends to be dispersed throughout the organization. (Each unit or brand may have its own finance, marketing, and IT leaders.) When this happens, the CMO often helps provide strategic leadership across the corporation. We frequently see this in global, multibrand firms where category or business unit managers have P&L responsibility. However, as the company gets larger and more complex, C-level roles often have to be disaggregated. This is no different for the CMO's role, which may get divided into several parts, such as chief commercialization officer, chief innovation officer, chief analytics officer, and so on. In contrast, when a firm has a

single brand or all of marketing is centralized, it's easier for the CMO to play an enterprise-wide role.

Step 2: Match Responsibilities to the Job's Scope

Once the CEO decides where a CMO ought to have an impact, the role's responsibilities should be aligned accordingly. Almost all CMOs are in charge of brand strategy and insight generation. CMOs with a strategic focus also need to oversee the firm's "think tank" efforts (which originate innovations and product designs) but have little to no responsibility for converting strategy into tactics such as ads or marketing communications. CMOs in a commercialization role should have extensive responsibility for developing and converting the brand strategy into marketing plans that drive sales (through social, digital, advertising, and content initiatives; events; partnerships; and so on) but little responsibility for up-front, firm-level strategic decisions. And CMOs in an enterprise-wide P&L role should have responsibility for the whole process.

Alignment of responsibilities is the critical area where mistakes are made. It's common for companies to describe a role in which the CMO is expected to change the overall performance of the firm, but when you examine the job duties closely, it's clear the CMO has only commercialization functions. In other words, expectations typically far exceed the actual authority given the CMO.

That problem is often compounded when CEOs are wooing candidates who already have good jobs. While overpromising and upselling are common in recruitment across many functions, our research suggests that they can be a bigger issue in marketing—because of the general confusion and lack of uniform

The riskiest job in the C-suite

The tenure of CMOs and other top executives.

Average years by industry	CEO	CFO	CIO	CMO	CHRO	C-suite
Consumer	8.0	5.1	4.5	3.6	4.9	5.2
Energy	6.1	5.0	4.5	4.6	5.3	5.1
Financial services	9.7	5.5	4.1	5.1	5.1	5.9
Industrials	6.7	4.9	4.0	4.1	4.6	4.9
Life sciences	9.4	6.0	4.1	3.1	5.1	5.5
Professional services	9.2	5.0	4.5	4.1	5.1	5.6
Technology	7.9	4.9	4.4	4.3	5.2	5.3
Overall average	8.0	5.1	4.3	4.1	5.0	5.3

Source: Korn Ferry, "Age and Tenure in the C-Suite," February 14, 2017, https://www.kornferry.com/about-us//press/age-and-tenure-in-the-c-suite-korn-ferry-institute-study-reveals-trends-by-title-and-industry.

expectations about what a CMO does and the knowledge and skill differences among marketing executives.

Step 3: Align Metrics with Expectations

Once the job's role and responsibilities have been nailed down, the CEO needs to define how the CMO's success will be measured.

A CMO in a well-designed commercialization role will be held accountable for meeting budgetary goals; for the outcomes of projects (such as a website redesign); for the results produced by marketing programs (for example, increased traffic to stores); and for management outcomes (like improved staff satisfaction and performance). In contrast, CMOs in strategy roles should be held accountable for related elements of firm performance, such as increases in revenue or same-store sales, in addition to meeting budgets and producing management outcomes. And of course, CMOs overseeing P&Ls should be measured on the top- and bottom-line business results (and on budgetary, project, and management outcomes).

This approach may sound like common sense, but it's surprising how infrequently it's followed. Only 22% of the job descriptions we studied mentioned how the CMO would be measured or held accountable, and only 2% had a specific section that clearly articulated job expectations. While 90% made some mention of expectations, they typically were vague. The head of marketing for one technology company, for example, was supposed to "help define and execute an aggressive growth strategy for the company." What exactly is the measure of success for that? Is it producing a strategic plan? Or some sort of growth target (and if so, how is it measured)? If metrics and goals aren't predetermined, how do CMOs know if they have hit their targets?

Step 4: Find Candidates with the Right Fit

Even when the CMO role is well defined, assessing candidates can be a challenge, because their training and experience vary so much. Marketers lack the professional certifications required of lawyers and accountants. Only 6% of CMOs we looked at in our research had degrees in marketing. Although 44% had MBAs, their educational backgrounds varied a lot. They included degrees in engineering, economics, mathematics, philosophy, political science, psychology, and other subjects. Consequently, the type of experience and training marketing executives gain during the formative part of their careers—and specifically, whether they have served primarily under CMOs in strategy, commercialization, or enterprise-wide P&L roles—will largely determine which roles they are best suited to later in their careers.

Another stumbling point, in our analysis, is that in almost all CMO job descriptions there are significant gaps between the responsibility given and the experience required. For instance, 39 of the job descriptions we studied indicated that the CMO would oversee product strategy but then neglected to require experience in that area. Sometimes the gaps ran in the other direction. Thirty-four of the descriptions required candidates to have direct-marketing experience even though the jobs didn't include any direct-marketing duties.

To understand how confusing this mismatch can be, consider the description for the CMO job at a top manufacturer. This firm wanted its head of marketing to lead the analysis of what drove customer preferences, develop a superior brand strategy, set the marketing strategy, and oversee implementation of those strategies. However, the actual position included responsibility only for a marketing insights group, a marketing project-management group, and a media group. The description led the reader to believe the CMO's role was far bigger than it actually was.

The problem didn't stop there. The description stated that candidates should have "best-in-class consumer-packaged-goods industry experience" (translation: P&L experience), demonstrated corporate/marketing strategy leadership, sales experience, and more. But the job involved neither P&L nor sales responsibilities, so these requirements made little sense. A better match for the job would have been someone with research and analysis skills, media and digital experience, and a proven ability to develop marketing programs that deliver in-market results. While the lack of internal consistency may seem obvious, few of the CEOs and CMOs we've interviewed recognize that a disconnect exists.

How to Improve Outcomes

Although CEOs express disappointment in their CMOs, they typically don't realize that they may have played a role in creating the problem. By making sure that the CMO job is designed and staffed correctly, they can increase their own satisfaction with their top marketing executive.

Before looking for a new CMO, a CEO should be sure to answer the following questions:

- What outcomes do we want the CMO to produce, particularly in light of the company's priorities? Which of the three CMO types do we need? How should this person balance out the management team's strengths (and weaknesses)?

- What functional responsibility is necessary to realize our vision for the role? Will that level of responsibility really work, given other top management team roles?

- What will success look like? What specific key milestones will the CMO be expected to reach?

- What types of skills and experience are required?

When considering this last question, too many CEOs describe someone who is the best athlete rather than the best player for the specific position. It's important to avoid that temptation. For their part, CMO candidates shouldn't view the job description as a fait accompli. In our surveys, CMOs who say their roles are correctly designed often had a hand in crafting them before accepting their jobs. That indicates how critical it is for CMOs to negotiate the specifics of their responsibilities and expectations.

Before signing on to any CMO position, a candidate should make sure they understand the following:

- What is really the CMO's role in the firm? Is there agreement about this across the C-suite? Do the CEO, CFO, CHRO, and the board all describe the position in the same terms?

- What is really the CMO's responsibility? Which functions report to the CMO on the org chart, and which don't? What departmental budget items are the CMO's responsibility? Are any budgetary areas missing? (Though some firms may balk at sharing budgets with candidates during the hiring process, asking to see them is valid and can serve as a test of whether the firm wants to be transparent about the position's responsibilities.)

- Are the expectations and performance metrics for the role consistent with the responsibilities and the candidate's experience? Is the CMO being set up to succeed?

After answering these questions, the candidate should summarize in writing their understanding of the role and the expectations and responsibilities involved with it, and share it with both the executive recruiter and the CEO, asking for confirmation that they are all on the same page.

Executive recruiters can use the following questions to guide the process:

- Does the CEO understand the range of CMO roles? Do they understand that the position should be designed before a job description is written? Have they anticipated how altering the CMO role might affect other C-suite leaders?

- Are expectations, responsibilities, and measures of success consistent with the chosen CMO role? Is that consistency clear in the written job description? Are the skills it outlines in keeping with those expectations and responsibilities, too?

- What type of CMO expertise is the best match for the role the firm has in mind?

- Have prospective CMOs been educated on the different types of roles and the degree to which their own background and skills fit the role in question? (Being open and honest about gaps in preparation for specific positions can help prospective CMOs anticipate challenges and identify experience they should gain.)

As experts in designing CMO roles, executive recruiters must lead, rather than follow, the CEO in talks about the role. But in our interviews with recruiters who focus on CMO placements, we came across only one who had a model for guiding CEOs through a discussion of how to design the right role for the firm. While everyone has a vested interest in helping new CMOs succeed, recruiters have an additional incentive to get it right, since their compensation is traditionally at risk if a candidate they place fails within the first year on the job.

Learning the Hard Way

Together, the authors of this article have spent eight years exploring why CMO hiring so often goes off track. But one of us—Kim—has personal experience with the challenges that result when the design of a CMO role hasn't been completely thought through.

Kim began her marketing career at Procter & Gamble, where marketers typically have P&L responsibility. As a result, she assumed that all C-level marketing jobs had it. Some years after leaving P&G, she interviewed for an exciting CMO position that the recruiter insisted would be "transformational." But in the first week at the new company, Kim realized to her surprise that she didn't have P&L authority. Instead of sitting in strategy-setting meetings, she was trying to figure out if advertising conformed to brand guidelines. This was not what she thought she'd signed up for.

Looking back, Kim made some mistakes that might now seem obvious. She focused on the job description and relied on the recruiter's assurances instead of asking the right questions during interviews. Had she asked to see org charts and budgets before accepting the company's offer, she would have quickly realized that the CMO's responsibility was much narrower than she thought. That would have enabled her to have a pointed discussion with both the executive recruiter and the CEO regarding the importance of role design.

To fix the situation, she worked to change the scope of and expectations for her job. After a couple of in-market wins, she partnered with the COO (who had P&L authority) to design a different role for marketing. She had a terrific CEO who believed that marketing should expand its duties and supported the change. Because the economy was in turmoil, the COO was more than happy to share accountability for financial performance. Over time the key players began expecting marketing to assume more P&L responsibilities, essentially changing the nature of the CMO role.

As Kim's story shows, it is possible to proactively change the scope of a CMO job after being hired. However, hiring mismatches aren't good for firms or their executives, and fixing them takes a lot of time and effort. Companies would be better off if CMOs spent their energy doing the jobs they were qualified for from the outset. Our hope is that our research will help CEOs and CMOs avoid this problem in the future. Everyone—C-suite executives, subordinates, and shareholders—will benefit if a company creates the right CMO role from the beginning and then finds the right kind of person to fill it.

Originally published in July–August 2017. Reprint S17041

Are Your Marketing and Sales Teams on the Same Page?

by Kelsey Raymond

Throughout the pandemic, businesses have needed to continuously adapt as customer needs and preferences evolve. But that quick adaptation is difficult when the business lacks alignment between the departments that most frequently speak to potential customers: sales and marketing.

When sales and marketing teams aren't aligned, both suffer. In fact, sales-marketing misalignment is estimated to cost businesses more than $1 trillion each year.[1] Why? This misalignment can lead to a lack of trust and understanding between the two departments, which makes every step of working together more difficult and therefore slower.

When businesses need to adapt their sales or marketing efforts quickly, misalignment that costs the company a day or two can mean big changes to business outcomes, such as fewer sales and lost revenue.

Identifying Alignment and Misalignment

Because of the potential impacts on revenue, it's important for business leaders to recognize what functional and dysfunctional sales-marketing alignments look like in practice.

Let's start by looking at misalignment around objectives. Imagine that a company's salespeople are having conversations with leads that enlighten them about their buyers' changing business operations—and the resulting new needs—but that the salespeople aren't sharing this information quickly with the marketing team. If the marketing team doesn't know about prospective customers' changing needs, they can't create content or campaigns to address these updated pain points. That means all the sales collateral is outdated.

Misalignment can stem just as easily from the marketing side of the equation. For example, a marketing team might have noticed that the website's blog posts addressing certain buyer pain points are spiking in traffic as people search for solutions online. But if they aren't communicating these trends to the sales team, the salespeople taking calls might not know to mention solutions for those fresh pain points—potentially losing buyers.

In both examples, the lack of communication and an effective feedback loop is causing both teams to lose opportunities—leading to fewer sales and less revenue for the organization.

When sales and marketing teams have a system for proper alignment, though, the company will notice a few key benefits:

- *Increased speed of change.* When two teams are aligned and collaborating regularly, it's easier to make strategic changes quickly. A consistent feedback loop means

Idea in Brief

The Problem

Sales and marketing misalignment is estimated to cost businesses more than $1 trillion each year.

The Solution

Synchronize the two functions using several strategies:

- Audit your content to identify redundancies and opportunities.
- Have marketing shadow sales calls.
- Hold regular brainstorming sessions with sales and marketing team members.
- Share knowledge about prospects for sales calls.

The Results

Greater marketing-sales alignment increases speed, trust, creative problem-solving, and employee retention, improving overall company performance.

that both teams have all the necessary context to hit the ground running on conversations about what they need from each other.

- *Creative problem-solving.* Often, people in sales and marketing roles have different perspectives and ways of thinking. When they are aligned on objectives, they'll contribute those different perspectives to help solve any problems that might arise, which can lead to more-creative solutions.

- *Employee retention.* Salespeople don't want to work where they lack support from marketing; they view that support as necessary to succeed in their roles. And marketers don't want to work where they don't receive respect from the sales team or where their hard work doesn't result in closed sales. Ensuring alignment, trust, and respect between these two departments makes it more likely that employees will want to continue working together.

Aligning Marketing and Sales

A whopping 90% of sales and marketing professionals report misalignment in terms of strategy, process, culture, and content in their organizations, and nearly all respondents of the same survey believe this harms the business and its customers.[2] What's more, 97% of those same respondents reported difficulties with messaging and content in particular; the top complaints included content created by marketing without the sales team's input, content focused on pushing products rather than solving leads' problems, and content that doesn't move prospects through the buyer's journey.

To combat these problems, companies can ensure the sales and marketing teams become (and remain) aligned on their shared objectives—and that marketing collateral supports the sales team's efforts—by implementing the following strategies.

1. Audit the content you have to enable revenue generation.

The pandemic has changed B2B buyers' behavior, with one-third of buyers spending more time on prepurchase research but one-quarter of buyers spending less time talking with vendors.[3] Sales and marketing teams need to think more strategically about the content they're sending B2B buyers about products and services, because buyers are relying more heavily on written information in their decision-making.

The first step in strategizing is to audit available sales-enablement content and how it's being used. First, take an inventory of your content stock, so you can avoid duplicating efforts. Make a note of what collateral you have and what content you lack by having your marketing and sales teams work together to answer the following questions:

- What content do you have now that does the heavy lifting in terms of sales enablement?

- What content is outdated and requires revisions?

- What questions do prospects and leads frequently ask the sales team?

- Who's reading the content currently—and who should be reading it? What content can you create to attract that desired audience?

- Should the sales team be more involved in lending their insights for content?

The goal is to map your content to your objectives so that you can see what's being used well, what's underused, and what content may not be meeting expectations. Then you can determine whether your sales and marketing teams need to realign their content strategy.

2. Have marketing team members shadow sales calls.

Cross-department shadowing, such as having marketing team members periodically shadow sales calls, can ensure that your sales and marketing teams are aligned. It can also spark topic ideas for great sales-enablement content.

Here's how you can implement this in your company:

- Ask marketing team members to listen to sales calls on a regular cadence, perhaps once a month.

- Invite the marketing team to the sales team's sales-call debrief meetings or other sales-related hangouts.

- Include sales-call shadowing in your training processes for new marketing hires.

Not only does this help the marketing team learn how they can best create campaigns to aid the sales team, it also allows sales teams to gain an outside perspective on their everyday work. The marketing team might be able to suggest more-relevant sales collateral to send leads, uncover gaps in the sales process, and even detect customer pain points the sales team hadn't considered. All of those insights can lead to a more streamlined sales process.

3. Hold regular brainstorming sessions with sales and marketing team members.

Another way to get sales and marketing into the same room is to schedule recurring brainstorming sessions. The brainstorming goal could be to discuss prospects, shore up gaps in the sales process, or develop topics for white papers or webinars. Regardless, set an agenda ahead of time so that both teams can prepare and bring relevant data points. During the sessions, you might discuss questions such as:

- What common questions do prospects ask during the sales process?

- What sales-related questions are time-consuming to answer?

- What are the common barriers to prospects moving forward in the sales process?

- What's the most common piece of content salespeople email to leads? What does the subject line say?

- What kinds of content do salespeople search for in our vault but fail to find?

- What verbiage has the sales team used about the company, product, or service that resonated with prospects?

The goal of these brainstorming sessions is to uncover insights that can help replicate wins and shake loose content ideas that will support future sales.

4. Provide the sales team with knowledge about prospects for their sales calls.

If your marketing team uses marketing automation software, they likely have a lot of information on prospective buyers that the sales team lacks. Create a process to allow the sales team to access key background information on the people they've booked phone calls with. The marketing team probably has information on leads that a salesperson would find valuable, including:

- *How the lead learned about the company.* Website form submissions often include this question, so it's a matter of extracting this information from the marketing automation software. Alternately, the sales team could see how the lead first arrived on the company's website (e.g., organic search, direct traffic, or a referral link).

The source will shed light on the lead's intent and possible readiness to buy.

- *What content the lead engaged with on your site before filling out a contact form or downloading a piece of content.* This can tell the sales team what solutions the prospect is most interested in and what topics they're already educated on, so the salesperson can prepare for the sales call accordingly.

- *What information the lead provided in a contact form.* This could include title, available budget, and company size.

Ultimately, getting sales and marketing aligned starts with instilling a shared culture of cooperation by creating processes that remind the teams of their joint objectives and that encourage mutual feedback. Doing so, you can avoid the sales-marketing misalignment that plagues so many organizations and forces them to leave so much money on the table.

Adapted from hbr.org, December 9, 2021. Reprint H06Q40

7

How AI Can Power Brand Management

by Julian De Freitas and Elie Ofek

F
ew brands are more iconic than Nike. From its swoosh logo to its slogan "Just Do It," the company has mastered the artistry necessary to build a renowned brand. So when Nike asked Obvious, a trio of Parisian artists who make AI-inspired designs, to develop new iterations of the Air Max sneaker in 2020, it wanted to be sure the designs wouldn't deviate too dramatically from Nike's signature style. Obvious trained its generative AI model by feeding it pictures of the Air Max 1, the Air Max 90, and the Air Max 97 and used the model to create a vast array of design ideas. Then, drawing on their own knowledge and perception of broader fashion trends along with Nike's marketing objectives, the trio iteratively tweaked the model until it produced a design that struck the right balance between novelty and staying on brand. The design incorporated many of the stylistic elements of the classic Air Max but blended them with new colors, shapes, and patterns to

achieve a fresh, cool feel. The limited-edition shoes sold out in less than 10 days.

Unsurprisingly, marketers have begun experimenting with AI to improve their brand-management efforts. But unlike other marketing tasks, such as A/B testing and bidding on search words, brand management involves more than just repeatedly executing one specialized function. Long considered the exclusive domain of creative talent, it encompasses multiple activities designed to build the reputation and image of a business—such as crafting and communicating the brand story, ensuring that the product or service and its price reflect the brand's competitive positioning, and managing customer relationships to forge loyalty. A brand is a promise to customers about the quality, style, reliability, and aspiration of a purchase. AI can't fulfill that promise on its own (at least not anytime soon). But it can help shape customers' impressions of a brand at every interaction. And it can automate expensive and complex creative tasks—including product design.

Mixing brands and automation is a delicate affair. AI has the potential to adversely affect a brand, so successfully implementing it in this context often involves confronting resistance and backlash from both customers and employees. Nevertheless, AI is becoming an integral part of brand management. To succeed with it, you must understand how it is perceived by stakeholders and what can be done not simply to mitigate their concerns but to make them avid supporters. You must be sure not to overautomate by removing any sense of human control or making AI the face of the brand. And you should always keep in mind that AI and creative pursuits aren't opposing forces.

On the basis of examples from Intuit, Caterpillar, LOOP, and Jasper AI, along with in-depth scholarly research, we propose a

Idea in Brief

The Opportunity

Brand management, long considered the exclusive domain of creative talent, has become faster and better informed than ever because of AI.

The Challenge

AI has the potential to adversely affect a brand, so successfully implementing it in this context often involves confronting resistance and backlash from both customers and employees.

The Solution

The most successful brand management blends the best of human and machine intelligence to augment rather than replace human creativity. Nike, Intuit, Caterpillar, and others have used AI to the great benefit of their brands.

framework for thinking about the key roles that AI plays when it comes to managing brands effectively. The most successful approaches blend the best of human and machine intelligence to augment, not replace, human creativity.

The Four Ps of AI's Brand Impact

AI can improve performance at each stage of the customer-management life cycle, from acquisition to development and even retention. Those performance improvements, in turn, can reinforce and extend a brand's equity. They can be grouped into four basic categories of impact: *Productivity*—AI increases the efficiency and convenience of accomplishing marketing tasks, improving the customer experience and driving brand loyalty. *Prediction*—AI reduces uncertainty, augmenting what the brand can promise and thereby building confidence and trust in the product and the company. *Personalization*—AI increases engagement and relevance for the firm's offering by tailoring elements to each customer, thus forging the image of a brand that cares about the customer's needs on an ongoing basis. *Proposals*—AI offers new creative solutions and value drivers while staying true to the brand's essence.

Although new forms of AI are constantly being developed, this framework accommodates the main roles that it can and will play. For example, classification algorithms, like the ones that sort for spam in your email, contribute to each of the first three Ps, whereas generative AI can contribute to all four and is especially suited to personalization and proposals. Brands should use this framework as a simple guide for navigating a complex and expanding industry. If an AI program doesn't contribute to any of the four Ps, it's probably not worth the risk to the brand associated with the technology.

Now let's dig deeper into the framework to see how some companies are already using artificial intelligence to improve their brand management.

1. Productivity

Customer service reps are your frontline brand ambassadors. And, arguably, the most important step in brand management is retaining expensively acquired and developed customers. The risk that a customer will be unable to resolve an issue with a product, a service, or a payment satisfactorily—and will then abandon the brand—is one of the biggest challenges a company faces.

When customers have problems, they contact customer support, and most would rather wait in line for a human agent than get help immediately from a chatbot. Their biggest complaints about bots are a lack of understanding and an inability to solve complex issues. However, unlike chatbots, humans are not eternally attentive, patient, and cheerful—especially when faced with a relentless queue of angry callers. Long wait times and frustrating interactions may corrode a company's brand and lead customers to depart.

Intuit, a global financial-technology platform that makes software for personal finance, small-business operations, and tax prep, offers products including TurboTax, Mailchimp, Credit Karma, and QuickBooks. At one point it was dealing with a barrage of customer questions and complaints regarding the use of its software. To improve its customer service, Intuit wanted to provide its agents with frequent feedback on their performance. But only about 10% of callers answered customer experience surveys (a typical response rate for call centers), and managers could listen in on only a small subset of calls. So agents had little opportunity to receive robust feedback in a timely manner.

To overcome that challenge, Intuit used transcripts of the calls that customers had rated to train an AI model to detect which interactions were most likely to result in customer satisfaction. Because all calls were recorded and could readily be transcribed, Intuit could use the trained AI model to provide personalized daily feedback to all its agents based on all calls, whether they'd been customer-rated or not.

Thus the company improved customer satisfaction at a fraction of the cost of typical human supervision or expensive training programs for its agents. And because the employees were more effective, they felt more fulfilled. Furthermore, because Intuit engaged employees at all levels and solicited their input on how to design a dashboard to display feedback for them, it eased concern that agents were going to be replaced by AI and ensured that they remained the face of the brand when customers called in to get support.

2. Prediction

Caterpillar, a maker of heavy-duty construction and mining equipment, uses AI to deliver additional value by literally foreseeing the future. Its subdistributor Borusan Cat, based in Turkey, faced this problem: When a customer's equipment broke down, the repairs were often very expensive because a part had deteriorated to the point where it damaged the rest of the machine. In some cases, an engine overhaul was needed, and the downtime to get the necessary parts and conduct the extensive repairs was costly for both the customer and Borusan Cat. Furthermore, when their machinery did break down, customers sometimes turned to unauthorized third-party vendors, resulting in lost business for Borusan Cat. The company believed that it could deliver significant value by detecting part failures before they rendered the equipment inoperable, much the way a medical checkup can detect a clogged artery and prevent a heart attack.

The first step was to establish the infrastructure necessary to harvest data. The company embedded sensors in the machines to continuously harvest information on the state and use of the machines' parts. After amassing enough failure incidents, the company trained AI to combine signals from various parts of the equipment with past data patterns to predict—with 97% accuracy—which piece of equipment was at risk of breaking down and what the exact problem would be. Using these predictions, the company alerted customers and selectively sent its technicians to validate diagnoses and determine the level of service or repair required. If the customer agreed, the equipment would be repaired with minimal if any downtime and more cheaply than if the customer had waited for the machine to malfunction.

However, despite the benefits of the AI-based technology, willingness to pay for its insights was initially lacking. Customers thought that proactive calls from technicians were a marketing gimmick to sell more parts or service. Salespeople were skeptical of the technology, especially when it flagged equipment on a "healthy" site that they had been unconcerned about. And because each repair was a low-ticket item compared with selling equipment, salespeople had little incentive to pursue repairs. For these reasons they were waiting too long to call customers whose machines had been flagged as being at risk of breaking down—thereby failing to deliver on the company's promise of preemptive maintenance and in the process doing damage to the brand.

After a few twists and turns, management chose to abandon the uphill battle of explaining the capabilities of the technology to skeptical customers. Instead it absorbed the value of the technology into its maintenance contracts. The company guaranteed customers no downtime, or else Borusan Cat would provide replacement equipment. Thus the AI's predictive capabilities augmented the brand's promise and also removed the possibility that customers would turn to third parties if their equipment broke down. The company captured the added value provided by the AI without drawing attention to its presence.

That fix also addressed the sales team's financial incentives. Folding AI insights into the maintenance contracts resulted in a higher-ticket sales item worth prioritizing. Because it was critical that salespeople follow up on AI alerts in a timely manner, the company also created a central, cross-organizational team dedicated to that service.

With those changes in place, the company could finally realize the technology's potential: to repair parts before they sustained significant damage. In fact, because the parts removed from repaired equipment were often salvageable, they could be refurbished and resold. Effectively providing these added services each time a repair was needed gave Borusan Cat more opportunities to interact positively with customers, increasing the attractiveness of its AI solution while reinforcing its image as a trustworthy brand that cares about customers' business and long-term success.

3. Personalization

Getting customers through the door is an achievement. But they may make only a single purchase, sign up for the most basic service, or buy a limited quantity of the company's products. In that case the company generates modest revenues from customers it expended considerable resources to acquire. And customers may become less excited about an offering over time and feel that they are overpaying—severely restricting their lifetime value.

To see how AI can enable a company to provide tailored offerings that keep existing customers engaged with the brand, let's turn to an unorthodox car-insurance app: LOOP. It doesn't use several standard insurance-premium criteria, such as credit score, income level, and occupation, which tend to introduce bias against certain minority groups. It can afford to omit them because, as an AI-powered smartphone app, it constantly collects risk-relevant data about where customers drive (type of road, traffic volume, weather) and how (speeding, hard braking, talking on a cell phone). Its unique approach combines that data with extensive information on road accidents to predict, using AI, whether a customer who tends to drive in a particular way on particular roads is at high, medium, or low risk of filing a claim. Using the AI's predictions, LOOP makes additional offerings to customers, including much cheaper rates. Just imagine how a LOOP customer feels when she receives a notification like this: "You're on a roll, Jacky! You've unlocked a surprise for driving safe: lower rates!" LOOP further incentivizes safe driving by providing a customized, continually updated driving score (say, 8.18 out of 10), along with safety insights and tips gleaned from its treasure trove of customer and road data combined with what it learns about individual drivers' behavior. Customers see, on a weekly basis, meaningful feedback and suggestions about how to drive and what roads to avoid—plus actual results in terms of their scores and rates. That goes a long way toward removing any skepticism they may have had about whether an insurance app that eschews many of the conventional measures can accurately assess their risk. Although several competitors offer customers some benefits in exchange for gaining access to their telematics data (typically only driving behavior), these are usually comparatively small discounts—and they employ the data more as an excuse to send users telemarketing communications than to set their rates.

LOOP not only helps create safer roads; it lowers the chances that its customers will get into an accident and file a claim, increasing their lifetime value. In short, AI helps achieve a win-win for the customer and the company while building the image of a brand that is fair and cares about customers' well-being beyond the initial point of sale.

4. Proposals (Lots of Them)

A brand has a unique tone or personality that cuts across all company communications, from social media and email messages to blogs and other long-form content. A well-defined and consistent brand voice reinforces brand image, fosters a deeper connection with the audience, and helps the brand stand out from competitors.

Many managers have resisted automating brand communications, despite the advent of large language models. First, they worry that using generative AI means surrendering their brand's unique voice in favor of generic, cookie-cutter output. Second, they are wary of the tendency of large language models to "hallucinate" facts in their responses, hurting a brand's reputation. Third, they are rightfully concerned that whatever they put into the system will be used to train the models and thus will become accessible to competitors. In short, they see a trade-off between marketing efficiency and staying in control of the brand's image and integrity.

Consider how Jasper AI, a marketing-content generator, navigates that trade-off. Let's say you want to create a marketing campaign. You begin by helping Jasper learn your brand's unique tone of voice. You can upload a style guide or link Jasper to a few examples of previous posts that you believe best reflect your brand. Jasper will learn your brand's personality (attitudes and feelings about a topic), style (word choice, sentence structure, rhetorical devices), and other aspects of the language you typically use in branded communications. For instance, it can learn that your brand's tone is more casual than formal, more funny than serious, or more irreverent than respectful. Then you upload information about your company, products, services, and audience, and the goal or objective of the communication.

Jasper will help generate marketing materials for communication campaigns. It will conjure a solid first draft of, say, a blog post that is not only optimized for search engine visibility but is also written in your brand's unique voice and accurately incorporates facts about your company. Beneath the hood, Jasper leverages a family of large language models (OpenAI, Bard, Stability.ai, and Anthropic) and searches Google for the latest news to ensure that its proposals are up to date, because most large language models have been trained on "old" data, perhaps to 2019. Most important, it layers facts about your business with your brand's distinctive qualities while ensuring that those facts are not used to train the underlying AI models.

You are involved throughout the process. You can ask Jasper to help you edit the blog to better align with your desired brand attributes (for example, "infuse more excitement," "convey a more upbeat attitude," "emphasize global appeal") or to keep generating entirely new blog posts until you see one you like. Jasper can also morph the blog into other types of marketing content for your campaign, such as a landing page, a LinkedIn post, or an email, creating a full gallery that conforms to the format of each asset type while preserving the essence of the brand. And if you need to replicate your campaign for a different product or audience (say, consumers in the developed world), simply upload information for that audience, switch out audiences in a drop-down menu, and let Jasper regenerate all the materials.

In these various ways Jasper can eliminate the trade-off between efficient marketing and controlling your brand identity, allowing you to creatively communicate at scale without losing your brand's distinctive voice, veering away from the facts, or giving up your trade secrets.

. . .

AI cannot and should not automate all aspects of brand management. Our examples emphasize the importance of integrating it into conventional marketing efforts without making it the face of the brand or relying on it so much that it usurps your control. It should complement rather than substitute for the roles that human brand builders play.

As Nike's partnership with Obvious proved, managers can combine human intelligence with artificial intelligence to push the boundaries of what their brands can do. Successful brand managers will be those who master bringing out the "art" in artificial intelligence.

Originally published in September–October 2024. Reprint R2405G

8

Attract New Customers Without Alienating Your Old Ones

by Ryan Hamilton and Annie Wilson

I n response to the intense pressure to grow, many companies seek new kinds of customers. A broader customer base seems as if it should always be good for business: more buyers mean more revenue and higher market share. The North Face followed this path to growth in the 2010s, for example, when it leaned heavily into streetwear to attract "urban explorers" alongside its traditional outdoor enthusiasts. After the company added the new customer segment, its revenue rose from $2.3 billion in 2015 to $3.6 billion in 2024.

But targeting a new segment doesn't always result in growth. Many companies experience serious challenges when the new customers have needs, values, preferences, or identities that differ from those of their current customers. Occasionally, it even backfires spectacularly as brands not only fail to win over the new buyers but also drive off their current ones. Instead of expanding the business, their efforts damage their image and lead to customer boycotts, dips in stock price, and reduced revenue.

Kohl's, for example, tried to lure younger and less-price-sensitive customers to its department stores in the 2010s by giving more floor space to relatively expensive merchandise from brands like Sephora and Babies "R" Us, shrinking its selection of store-branded clothing to make room. Unfortunately, by changing itself to appeal to hypothetical new customers, Kohl's made itself less appealing to its dependable old ones: The chain's loyalists weren't happy that the low-priced items they wanted had been trimmed to make way for higher-priced things they didn't. From 2018 to 2025 the company's revenue fell by 20%, and its stock price plummeted by 89%. From 2021 to 2024 Kohl's changed its CEO twice.

Lands' End, Etsy, Sephora, Bud Light, WeightWatchers, and Starbucks are also among the brands that have faced a backlash after attempts to woo new customers. Some of them were able to successfully manage their way back into the good graces of their traditional customers while others proved decidedly less successful. But the overarching story is the same: Anytime a brand grows—or tries to grow—by attracting new segments, it risks creating conflict with the old ones. And the larger a brand gets, the more heterogeneous its customers will become, increasing the likelihood that tensions will arise.

Avoiding that problem—or solving it when it does emerge—requires a deeper understanding of the relationships between customer segments.

In our academic research, case studies, and consulting work with brands across diverse industries, we've discovered that there are four basic ways that customer segments relate to each other. In this article we'll introduce these types of relationships,

Idea in Brief

The Problem

Brands often pursue growth by attracting new customer segments. But if those newcomers differ too much from core customers, a brand can face a backlash—alienating its loyal base, inciting conflict, and harming its reputation and revenue.

The Solution

Understanding how customer segments interact can help. There are four types of relationships between segments: separate communities, connected communities, leader-follower segments, and incompatible segments. Companies can shift incompatible customers to another type of relationship to avoid or resolve conflicts. They can do this through separation, the creation of hierarchies, or, when needed, the firing of customer groups.

The Payoff

By managing segment conflicts, brands can grow more deliberately, avoid self-inflicted harm, and build stronger, more sustainable relationships that mutually reinforce the value of the brand.

show how conflict arises from them in predictable ways, and then describe how to identify and eliminate that conflict. These tactics work whether your company is proactively seeking to avoid clashes or is already waist-deep in them and needs a way out of the morass.

How Customer Segments Relate

Two key factors govern the nature of the relationship between segments. The first is whether the *value* each segment seeks from the brand is unique and independent (what we call *divergent* value) or depends on the use of the brand by another segment (what we call *collaborative* value). Customers who buy Timberland boots to wear to their blue-collar jobs, for example, and customers who stylishly pair them with fashionable jeans to wear on city streets are seeking divergent value. In contrast, eBay's buyer and seller segments get collaborative value because the platform becomes worth more to each segment the more the other uses it.

The second factor is the *sensitivity* of the segments to other types of customers. Some are *indifferent*: People who use John Deere tractors for heavy-duty farm chores are unfazed by the suburbanites who buy lawn mowers. But some brand users are *influenced* by each other—for good or ill. Beats headphones became popular among the masses because many musicians and athletes were seen wearing them. The association of Burberry with "chav" (antisocial, working-class youth) culture, however, turned off its posh customers. When the brand's nova check design became popular with football hooligans and soap stars, "it encapsulated everything that was bad about the brand or 'the wrong people' buying the brand," Siân Weston, the author of a history of Burberry, wrote.

These two factors combine in four ways to create the basic relationship types in our framework: *separate communities* (divergent and indifferent), *connected communities* (collaborative and indifferent), *incompatible segments* (divergent and influenced), and *leader-follower segments* (collaborative and influenced). (See the exhibit "The Four Types of Relationships Between Customer Segments.")

While most of the conflict emerges in the incompatible segments quadrant, it's important to understand the other three relationship types as well because they offer opportunities for brands to grow by adding new segments without conflict. Understanding how segments relate to each other will help you make key decisions such as which segment to target next and

The four types of relationships between customer segments

Customer segments tend to relate to each other in four different ways. Understanding how your segments interact can help you avoid conflict between them—or resolve it when it does emerge.

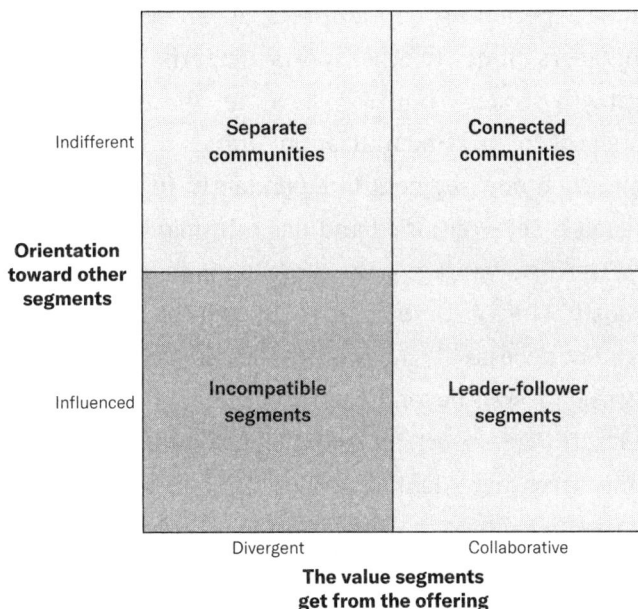

		Divergent	Collaborative
Orientation toward other segments	Indifferent	Separate communities	Connected communities
	Influenced	Incompatible segments	Leader-follower segments

The value segments get from the offering

which products and services will make growth least risky and most sustainable.

Separate communities

These segments value disparate things in a brand and its offerings, and each can seek its respective value without stepping on the toes of the other. Take Nike: Its segment of runners wants innovative running shoes worn by elite track stars and apps that can be used to log runs and facilitate race training. Meanwhile, the basketball segment wants basketball footwear and to see people like Caitlin Clark and LeBron James in the brand's ads. The fact that runners buy Nike Alphafly shoes doesn't affect basketball players shopping for Jordans; Nike customers get the value they want from the brand regardless of whether it offers products, experiences, digital assets, advertisements, or celebrity endorsers unique to other sports under the Nike umbrella.

A growth strategy built on separate communities has the advantage of compartmentalization: Brands can grow simply by courting each new segment independently, in a serial fashion, since each is self-contained and has minimal influence on the others. The disadvantage is that growing in this way can be relatively costly, since each segment requires its own marketing mix (though not necessarily its own product line), and the potential for organic growth beyond each community is limited. When Nike targets a new sport, for example, it typically invests significant resources and talent in developing sport-specific offerings and marketing approaches, which often include unique communication tactics and new distribution channels.

Connected communities

In this type of relationship, the brand becomes more valuable as more customers use it, even when those additional users come from other segments. Social media platforms like Instagram, two-sided markets like LinkedIn and eBay, and shared platforms like Venmo and Microsoft Windows all have segments that relate as connected communities. For example, various kinds of customers use LinkedIn to job hunt, to recruit, to network, to brag, and to share opinions. Because of network effects, the value the platform provides to all those segments increases as more people join it, but the customers in each segment are indifferent to who those other people are.

Connected community relationships offer brands the opportunity to multiply their growth as users attract more users. But they can also lead to catastrophic collapse when one or more segments start abandoning the brand. Within four months of its launch, in 2013, the video-sharing platform Vine had become the fastest-growing app in the world, with more than 200 million users. But its demise was fast as well. When the top content producers (one key segment) started leaving the network for more-lucrative platforms, many of Vine's ad buyers (another key segment) left as well. Growth began to slow in early 2016, and by July half of Vine's creators had either deleted their accounts or stopped posting. By October the company's parent, Twitter, announced that Vine would be shut down.

Leader-follower segments

This relationship is hierarchical. Leader segments have higher status than follower segments—whether they're cooler, more expert, or more authentic. (They don't need to be more numerous, however. Sometimes the follower segment vastly outnumbers and outspends the leader segment.) When leaders use a brand's offerings, it attracts people who want to emulate them.

A leader-follower strategy can be a cost-efficient way to acquire multiple segments: When leaders become customers, followers often find their own way to the brand. Leaders can serve as evidence of a brand's credibility, quality, trendiness, or cachet. For example, many home chefs seek out the cookware brand Le Creuset because of its association with professional chefs.

While a leader segment can include paid influencers, it cannot be made up exclusively of endorsers bought by the brand. To be effective it must include real consumers who demonstrate an authentic preference for or loyalty to the brand. When the Prius launched, the celebrities who drove the cars were an actual customer segment for Toyota, if a small one—the company wasn't handing out cars to everyone with a sitcom contract. All those tabloid photos that included a Prius made the odd-looking little hybrid slightly cooler to other potential customers.

The risk with a leader-follower strategy is that a leader segment could abandon the brand, since followers tend to go out the door right after them. Consequently, when brands serve leader-follower segments, it's crucial that they maintain their association with the leader segment and not become too focused on followers. Often brands shift their attention to the followers because they're more numerous or bring in more revenue than leaders do. But that approach could end up repelling both leaders and followers.

For example, as Carhartt has become a fashion brand, it has been careful to keep its focus on the blue-collar workers who form the core of its leader segment, continuing to target its marketing to them so that the follower segments of college kids, outdoor enthusiasts, and celebrities trying to look more relatable all benefit from Carhartt's perceived authenticity. If Carhartt started producing low-quality, fast-fashion garments or featuring its fashion segment more heavily in brand communications, it would risk turning off its blue-collar customers, potentially threatening its growth in both segments.

Incompatible segments

This is the relationship most prone to conflict. Incompatible segments derive different kinds of value from a brand's offerings, but because they influence each other, they're unable to comfortably coexist—like the core customers of Kohl's and the new, more affluent segment it desired. Intersegment conflict wreaks havoc on brands. Brands should steer clear of trying to serve customer segments that are incompatible.

Sources of Segment Tensions

To avoid or resolve a conflict, strategists and brand managers must first understand where it comes from. Then they can choose the solution that best addresses the problem. (It can also help to understand how vulnerable your business is—see the sidebar "Assessing the Risks of Segment Conflict.")

Functional conflict

This occurs when one customer segment impedes another segment's ability to enjoy a brand's products or services. Take Starbucks, which has grappled with functional conflict many times during its history.

The coffee chain initially attracted a large segment of customers who valued its relaxed "third place" atmosphere. Its shops were a place to unwind, read a newspaper, send a few emails, or catch up with a friend. But as its retail footprint increased, Starbucks began to attract large numbers of a different kind of customer: commuters who wanted a convenient place to grab a quick coffee rather than somewhere to linger over a handcrafted beverage. The commuters and the "third placers" clashed because they sought fundamentally different experiences. Long lines of impatient on-the-go customers rushing to get in and out made the coffee shops uninviting for third placers. And conversely, too many customers ordering complicated specialty drinks in no hurry at all slowed down the lines and made it harder to find

Assessing the Risks of Segment Conflict

Certain features of a brand, its customer base, or the marketplace can make clashes between customer segments more likely or more consequential. Below are some key factors to examine.

Your Customers' Requirements

Too often brands define their segments in terms of demographic characteristics and not needs, preferences, and desires. But segments conflict when they *value* different things about a brand or its offerings, so it's essential to understand segments in those terms.

For example, should a brand that sells primarily to Millennials worry if it starts attracting Gen Z customers? Millennials aren't natural enemies of Gen Z, so probably not, but what if Millennial customers were seeking the brand's symbolic value of maturity, sophistication, and independence? If the Gen Z customers the brand attracted seemed immature, unsophisticated, or dependent in the eyes of those Millennials, then it's possible that they could cause conflict.

Your Brand Image

Brands with a narrowly defined, concrete image, brands that are positioned around exclusivity, and brands that are closely associated with a limited set of offerings or usage occasions tend to be at greater risk of inciting conflict as they acquire new segments. That's because introducing a new segment often challenges the brand's perceived meaning or makes it seem less exclusive. In contrast, brands that define themselves more broadly or abstractly or that sell a wide assortment of products, as Nike, Honda, and Apple do, are at less risk of creating conflict when they grow. Those brands don't have rigid boundaries for consumers to squabble over. While the risk is never zero, additional segments that purchase from abstract or inclusive brands tend to be less threatening to current customers.

Your Marketplace

Brands competing in highly competitive markets with many substitute offerings and low switching costs need to be very sensitive to the risks of conflict. Brands in less competitive markets, on the other hand, can often ride out low levels of conflict between customer segments.

The customer boycott that Bud Light experienced in response to its partnership with a transgender influencer was devastating—in part because of how easy it was to substitute one beer for another. In contrast, the National Football League, an entertainment property for which there is no direct substitute, regularly risks low levels of conflict in the name of expanding its customer base. Whether it's deciding to embrace Taylor Swift and her legions of new Chiefs fans or to run an ad with the tagline "Football is gay" in support of Carl Nassib, its first openly gay player, the NFL knows its fans will tolerate some level of conflict with fans who have different preferences and values in order to keep watching their favorite teams.

a place to park outside stores. Each segment hindered the ability of the other to get the functional benefits it sought. (We'll get to the solutions Starbucks came up with in the next section.)

Brand-image conflict

People buy a brand's offerings for more than just their utility; the brand's image also is a source of value and self-expression. When a brand attracts a new segment or makes changes to try to do so, it can threaten the authenticity, credibility, or purpose of the brand for other customers.

Tiffany & Co. faced a brand-image conflict when its relatively less expensive silver jewelry became popular among younger, less affluent consumers in the 1990s. While sales of the bracelets, charms, and necklaces drove significant revenue for the company, their lower prices and flocks of buyers threatened Tiffany's exclusive, high-end image for its core customers. If Tiffany became known as the go-to brand for gifts of silver baubles by high school sweethearts, could it still serve as a mark of elegance, extravagance, and sophistication for its wealthy customers? Its ultimate decision to raise prices on silver jewelry and introduce more-expensive collections suggests it thought not.

User-identity conflict

Brands frequently become associated with specific groups of users. Sometimes this happens because of a brand's functional properties—as it did with creatives who gravitated toward Apple products because of their superior design tools. Sometimes it happens for more-symbolic reasons, such as when a large number of hipsters started drinking Pabst Blue Ribbon beer to signal their authenticity. Once these associations are established, brands often become symbols of consumers' identification (or nonidentification) with certain groups. If people want to signal their interest in snowboarding, they wear Burton rather than Arc'teryx. If they want to show that they're real outdoorspeople, they use Yeti coolers rather than Igloo.

User-identity conflict arises if people in one customer segment think they can no longer use the brand to reliably signal their affiliation with a particular group because another segment has become associated with the brand. Take Supreme, a skateboard brand that really started to take off when it began attracting fashionable streetwear enthusiasts. To make itself more appealing to the new segment, Supreme partnered with luxury brands like Louis Vuitton and Rimowa. In doing so it stopped being a reliable symbol for the skateboarder community, which feared that it would be unclear whether someone carrying a Supreme backpack or wearing a T-shirt with the company's logo was truly a skater—or was just trying to buy a connection with that subculture. In 2023, after the skater segment started to turn on the brand, Supreme's year-over-year sales fell by nearly $40 million, or 7%, dropping from $562 million to $523 million.

Brand-image conflict and user-identity conflict often happen simultaneously, since customer identity often influences brand image. But they can also occur independently. In the case of Tiffany, for example, the problem was not that the traditional customers feared getting confused with or associated with the younger, more-price-sensitive customers (so there was no real risk of user-identity conflict) but that what the brand meant would start to change (brand-image conflict).

Ideological conflict

This occurs when a segment has values or beliefs that differ from or clash with those of another segment. Not all brand purchases are ideologically motivated, of course. Honda Accords are bought by people of nearly every political faction, nationality, and religion without causing any strife. So are iPhones, Big Macs, and HP printers. But increasingly, customers are seeking to align their purchases with their ideology, and when a brand endorses a certain viewpoint—or aligns itself with a segment identified with a certain viewpoint—it can create tensions.

Bud Light's hiring of the trans influencer Dylan Mulvaney in 2023 was intended to show its support for the LGBT community and attract younger customers. But that move was at ideological odds with its more politically conservative core customers. The result was a boycott that led to a 20% year-over-year decline in sales and dislodged Bud Light from its 20-year reign as the best-selling beer in America.

Avoiding and Resolving Conflicts

Escaping conflicts between customer segments most often requires nudging them into either a separate-communities relationship or a leader-follower relationship. Occasionally, it requires the difficult decision to jettison one of the segments completely. (Forward-looking brands can use these same strategies to tamp down conflicts before they ignite.) The right approach often depends on the source of the conflict.

Separate the segments

This is the most common approach for resolving conflicts. It can give each segment the space it needs to get what it wants from the brand without rubbing other segments the wrong way. Brand managers can create that distance by employing several tactics—perhaps simultaneously if the conflict is severe.

Using multiple communications channels, each targeting a different segment with customized content, is a popular strategy. For example, the North Face's main Instagram account (@thenorthface) is geared toward wilderness enthusiasts. But the brand also maintains accounts for those interested in specific outdoor sports (@thenorthface_climb and @thenorthface_snow), as well as several fashion-oriented accounts (@thenorthface_city and @thenorthface.purplelabel).

Brands can also turn down the heat through product development and differentiation. As we've noted, Timberland boots are popular with both blue-collar workers and fashionistas. But the brand has developed its Pro line to better serve the workers with more-rugged offerings while creating club-appropriate purple and pink versions of its boots for its stylish segment.

Sometimes the design of physical spaces or websites can create barriers between segments. Starbucks has developed different store formats to serve its different customer segments. There are still Starbucks locations with comfy chairs and workspaces for those who use coffee shops as third places, while kiosks and drive-through locations cater to the on-the-go segment. More recently, Starbucks introduced Reserve Roastery bars, upscale cafés with specially trained master baristas that are intentionally placed in out-of-the-way locations, to attract coffee connoisseurs back to the brand. The variety of store types encourages segments to select the space that serves them best, reducing functional conflict.

Separating customer segments isn't effective for all types of conflict, however. Different product lines and distribution channels tend to work well for reducing functional conflict. Subbrands can help with brand-image and user-identity conflict. But creating space—physical or conceptual—between segments often is not enough to address an ideological conflict.

Define leaders and followers

Creating or reestablishing a hierarchy among consumers can turn a previously incompatible relationship into a leader-follower relationship.

One way to do this is through subbrands, which can demarcate the status between customer groups. For example, Levi Strauss & Co. serves its core customer segment under its flagship Levi's brand. Customers who wear the original Levi's jeans are leaders who make the brand appealing to less affluent consumers who want to be like them because they're cooler, wealthier, and more fashionable. To give these followers access to the brand without diluting its image, the company sells more-affordable jeans under the label Signature by Levi Strauss & Co. (created in 2003 and available at Walmart).

The company distinguishes its offerings visually with distinct patches and colored tabs on waistbands and pockets. The brand's iconic red tab, which was first affixed to its jeans in 1936, is conspicuously missing on the lower-priced line.

In 2025, Levi Strauss added a new leader segment above the Levi's consumers by launching the Blue Tab Collection. This premium line of Japanese selvage denims with blue tabs on the pocket has prime leader and aspirational status. In the next tier are products with red tabs, which are followed by those with no tabs.

Subbrand hierarchies like these also reduce the risk of user-identity conflict. While the buyers of Signature might not care if Levi Strauss sold all types of jeans under a single brand, the fashion-oriented segments—who often value exclusivity and distinctiveness—could be turned off by that. Even something as simple as a colored tab the size of a fingernail can reduce conflict by creating a status ladder for segments.

Pricing and availability can also establish a hierarchy. Many Ferrari fans, for example, are followers who buy branded hats, sweatshirts, and collectibles but cannot afford the cars that the leader segment buys. Other brands provide additional services or a superior experience to their leaders. The Home Depot avoids intersegment conflict by offering its professional-tradespeople segment (leaders) additional services like dedicated checkout registers, inventory tracking via an app, and a special loyalty program not available to casual do-it-yourselfers (followers).

In these cases, the explicit hierarchies created by different product and service lines mitigate brand-image conflict as well as user-identity conflict. Unless Ferrari starts creating cheaper car models, its core customer base is unlikely to mistake some-one wearing Ferrari sunglasses for a true Ferrari car owner. For the Home Depot, the separate services help protect the brand's image as the go-to professional home-improvement store. By offering its Pro services, the retailer can still serve its segment of novice do-it-yourselfers without seeming as if it has lost its professional edge.

Fire a segment

This approach can be painful because it means forgoing the revenue that a segment brings in. But sometimes the long-term risk of losses from unresolved conflict makes the trade-off worthwhile. If the continued use of a brand by one segment makes it difficult for the brand to attract or retain other, more-valuable customers, it's often wise to nudge that segment toward the door.

In 2022 the amusement park company Six Flags sharply raised its ticket prices and eliminated most discount-ticket programs. When attendance dropped by more than 20% and revenue fell as a result, its CEO at the time, Selim Bassoul, countered the outcry by explaining that the move was deliberate. Many discount-ticket buyers spent little on high-margin refreshments and souvenirs, so they didn't generate much revenue. Further, by accommodating so many of those customers, Six Flags was creating a less enjoyable experience for everyone else and causing functional conflict: the result was overcrowding, longer wait times, and increased incidents of violence and theft. The price increase was designed to discourage rowdy teens with little to spend and produce a better experience for families willing to spend more.

Bassoul's vindication came in 2023, less than a year after the price hikes, when attendance at Six Flags was down but revenue reached a record high. The company's stock price soared by 20% as investors warmed to the strategy. The brand escaped functional conflict by firing one segment to better serve a more profitable crowd.

It's worth noting that there are times when brands knowingly stir up conflict in order to reinforce their values or to pursue a larger strategic aspiration. For example, when NASCAR banned Confederate flags from races in 2020, it most likely knew the move might create an ideological conflict with some longtime fans. But NASCAR hoped that in the long term it would have a net positive effect, attracting many new customers who would appreciate the explicit statement of values and feel more welcome at NASCAR events. *Sesame Street* also stepped into an ideological conflict when it showed Elmo receiving a Covid vaccine in 2022. Having been attacked by political conservatives for some decisions in the past, the organization was most likely aware that this pro-vaccine content wouldn't be received happily by all parents, but it chose to create conflict anyway in pursuit of a larger educational mission.

Still, examples of brands benefiting from conflict are more the exception than the rule. In most cases it's best to avoid it between customer segments.

. . .

Practical as we hope our advice may be, we want to be clear that managing customer relationships is not a matter of simply checking tasks off a list. What we're proposing is a wholesale reevaluation of the way brands think about growth. The conventional view of customer segments as independent growth targets is outdated. Brands need to recognize how those segments interact to create and destroy value.

Understanding customer relationships can help companies avoid land mines. But it can also help brands find opportunities if they look diligently. Either way, it's by acknowledging the interdependencies between customer segments that firms can facilitate lasting growth.

Originally published in July–August 2025. Reprint R2504H

Does Influencer Marketing Really Pay Off?

by Fine F. Leung, Jonathan Z. Zhang,
Flora F. Gu, Yiwei Li, and
Robert W. Palmatier

I n 2022, the influencer industry reached $16.4 billion.[1] More than 75% of brands have a dedicated budget for influencer marketing, from Coca Cola's #ThisOnesFor campaign, in collaboration with fashion and travel influencers, to Dior's award-winning 67 Shades of Skin campaign, where the brand partnered with diverse influencers to promote its Forever Foundation product line.[2] But does investing in influencers really pay off?

To explore this question, we collaborated with an international influencer marketing agency to analyze more than 5,800 influencer marketing posts on the popular Chinese social media platform Weibo.[3] (We focused our analysis on the Chinese market as home to one of the world's most sophisticated influencer marketing industries, but our findings are likely applicable in many other global markets.) The posts in our dataset were written by

What drives influencer marketing ROI?

A recent analysis identified seven key variables that impact engagement.

Influencer characteristic	Effect on ROI
1. Number of followers	⬆ +9.2%*
2. Posting frequency	⊖ Goldilocks effect**
3. Follower-brand fit	⊖ Goldilocks effect**
4. Originality	⬆ +15.5%*

Post characteristic	Effect on ROI
5. Positivity	⊖ Goldilocks effect**
6. Includes link to brand	⬆ +11.4%
7. Announces a new product	⬇ −30.5%

*Change in ROI corresponding to a one-standard-deviation increase.
**The highest ROI was achieved with a medium level of these characteristics—not too little, not too much.

2,412 influencers for 861 brands across 29 product categories, at costs ranging from $200 to almost $100,000 per post. And indeed, we found that on average, a 1% increase in influencer marketing spend led to an increase in engagement of 0.46%, suggesting that the strategy can in fact yield positive ROI.

However, we also found that most companies leave considerable value on the table: The average firm in our dataset could have achieved a 16.6% increase in engagement simply by optimizing how they allocated their influencer marketing budgets. Specifically, we documented the effects of seven key variables on influencer marketing ROI (see "What drives influencer marketing ROI?").

Idea in Brief

The Opportunity

Influencer marketing is a huge industry—generating more than $16 billion in 2022.

The Problem

Over 75% of brands have a dedicated budget for influencer marketing, but the authors of this article found that most companies are leaving substantial value on the table.

The Solution

By optimizing seven elements of any influencer campaign, including post frequency, originality, and positivity, brands can increase average engagement—and ROI—by 16% or more.

Below, we explore how firms can optimize each of these seven influencer campaign elements to potentially reach an average increase in engagement of more than 16%.

1. Number of followers

Unsurprisingly, we found that the more followers an influencer has, the more impactful a partnership will be. An influencer with a large following not only has a greater reach but is also seen as more popular and credible, generating higher engagement rates than brands would achieve by spending the same budget on partnering with a less popular influencer. In our dataset, posts from influencers whose follower bases were one standard deviation larger than average achieved 9.2% greater ROI.

2. Posting frequency

When it comes to how frequently an influencer posts, our analysis identified a Goldilocks effect: Influencers who post infrequently are seen as less informed sources of information. They also don't have enough presence on followers' feeds to build intimacy and trust. On the other hand, posting too frequently can clutter followers' feeds and create fatigue. Followers may become uninterested in the influencers' posts, selectively filter them, or even feel annoyed by them. As a result, brands that achieved the highest ROI partnered with influencers who had a medium level of posting activity, numbering around five posts per week.

Our analysis also suggests that many marketers may not realize the importance of this effect. Quite a few firms in our dataset worked with influencers who posted too rarely: We found that the companies could have increased the ROI of their influencer marketing efforts by an average of 53.8% simply by selecting influencers who engaged in the optimal level of posting activity.

3. Follower-brand fit

We found a similar Goldilocks effect regarding follower-brand fit, or alignment between the interests of an influencer's followers and a brand's domain. For example, follower-brand fit would be high if a skin care brand worked with an influencer whose followers were interested in beauty but low if it worked with someone whose followers were interested in automobiles. When an influencer's followers are highly interested in topics related to the sponsor brand, their posts tend to be more aligned with their followers' interests, making the posts more likely to feel personally relevant. But this also means that these posts will compete for followers' attention with a lot of similar content, so followers may lose interest in the topic. We found that partnering with influencers whose followers had some (but not too much) brand fit led to the best results.

From our analysis, the optimal level of follower-brand fit occurs when about 9% of an influencer's followers have interests that match with the sponsor brand; a difference of one standard deviation from this optimal level decreased ROI by 7.9%. Interestingly, most of the brands in our dataset were already engaging in near-optimal partnerships, suggesting that marketers may have some intuition for the benefits of medium follower-brand fit.

4. Influencer originality

The final influencer characteristic we examined was originality. While some influencers share a lot of content created by other people or brands, others largely post their own original content. Influencers who post a greater proportion of original content tend to stand out more, attract more attention, and appear more knowledgeable and authentic. As a result, we found that brands that partnered with these influencers typically achieved higher engagement rates for a given marketing spend. Specifically, we measured the proportion of an influencer's past posts that comprised original content and found that posts from influencers whose originality rates were one standard deviation higher than the average achieved 15.5% greater ROI.

5. Post positivity

One of the trickiest elements of any marketing campaign is tone. Marketers want to convey a positive message, but too much positivity can backfire—and this is just as true for influencer marketing as it is for more-traditional channels. Consumers are more likely to engage with highly positive posts, because they suggest a stronger endorsement. But if a post is so positive that it comes across as disingenuous, consumers may not react well.

For example, the following post from an Audi influencer uses a highly positive tone:

> *The #NewAudiQ2L is priced at RMB 217,700 to 279,000. It fully meets your travel needs with its great appearance, high technology, and high-efficiency power, and it brings a brand-new experience to young and free-spirited consumers. Click on the link to participate in the event, and you may win the chance to drive an Audi Q2L for one year!*

This post demonstrates the danger of excessive positivity: It cost the brand more than $4,000, and yet it wasn't reposted a single time! In contrast, the following post from a Clinique influencer exemplifies a more effective, medium-positivity tone; it had a lower price tag and yet achieved substantial engagement:

> *Yesterday a friend asked me what happened to my face these last two days? I looked so bad! I couldn't battle the smog of the changing seasons, and I didn't do a good job at skin maintenance, so dullness and fine lines appeared. I need to do something to nourish my skin! This year's new purple vitamin A "micro-needle tube" essence works really well. It contains pure vitamin A retinol, which can promote skin metabolism and collagen generation to fill in the fine lines.*

We also found that many firms had at least some room for improvement in this area: The posts in our dataset tended to be slightly more positive than optimal, to the point that reducing positivity could have helped these brands boost ROI by an average of 1.9%.

6. Including links to the brand

Consistent with prior research on content marketing, we found that posts that included links to a brand's social media account or external web pages performed significantly better.[4] This is because these links offer important additional information about the content, making consumers more likely to engage. In our dataset, posts that included links to a brand's website or social media achieved 11.4% higher ROI.

7. Announcing a new product

It may be tempting to turn to influencers when promoting a new-product launch, but our research suggests that this can be a counterproductive approach: We found that ROI for influencer posts announcing new products was 30.5% lower than for equivalent posts that were not about new-product launches. For example, this product-launch post from a Dyson influencer didn't perform very well:

> *Congratulations Dyson! Released a series of new smart home products. Desk lamps, air purifying heaters, vacuum robots! Technology brings more convenience and better health to our lives!*

But this post from a Kiehl's influencer—which was not about a new-product launch and which cost the brand less than a tenth of what Dyson paid for its post—achieved more engagement:

> *Kiehl's ultra-moisturizing cream must be a recommended product for life. It's the legendary best-selling moisturizing cream that has been ranked No. 1 for 40 years!*

Of course, all these recommendations are based on averages across our dataset, and results may vary for particular companies. In addition, our main metric for ROI was reposts, or shares. We chose this metric because reposts indicate greater engagement than more-passive forms of online interaction, such as simply "liking" a post, but they are by no means the only way to measure a campaign's success. And while short-term ROI can guide short-term decisions, brands should also consider the potential long-term effects of associating with a particular influencer. These effects (whether positive or negative) may take time to materialize, but they can have a substantial impact on a brand's identity.

That said, our analysis yields several tactical recommendations to optimize near-term engagement: When selecting an influencer, brands should look for partners with large follower bases, who post frequently (but not too frequently), who post a lot of original content, and whose followers' interests have some (but not too much) overlap with the brand's domain. And when developing posts, brands should strike a medium-positive tone, include links when possible, and avoid focusing on new-product launches. With these research-backed guidelines in mind, brands can move past anecdotal evidence to ensure that their marketing dollars go toward the partnerships and content that are most likely to offer returns.

Adapted from hbr.org, November 4, 2022. Reprint H07CSY

9

The Right Way to Build Your Brand

by Roger L. Martin, Jann Schwarz, and Mimi Turner

More than a century ago the merchant John Wanamaker wryly complained, "Half the money I spend on advertising is wasted. The trouble is, I don't know which half." Because the proponents of advertising have always struggled to prove that the money is well spent, that indictment has long helped financial executives justify cutting ad budgets. As no less an authority than Jim Stengel, a former chief marketing officer at Procter & Gamble, has noted, the struggle continues, although huge resources go toward testing advertising copy and measuring effectiveness.

The battle has become tougher with the advent of online advertising and "performance marketing"—that is, spending to capture and convert potential demand that has already arrived (for whatever reason) at the top of a brand's sales funnel. In other words, the advertiser pays for clicks. However, in what is now called "brand advertising"—designed to help establish awareness for a brand, a product, or a service to strengthen identity and increase customer loyalty—the link between advertising spending and positive financial outcomes is more tenuous. The result is that would-be brand builders face the dual challenge of Wanamaker's long-standing critique and the rise of performance marketing as a perceived legitimate alternative. The CEO of an iconic fashion clothing brand told one of us recently, "I am finding it impossible in my own organization, which notionally I control, to protect brand advertising against performance advertising spending."

We finally have an answer for Wanamaker—and a coherent rationale for investment in brand building. We drew on a large database supplied by the World Advertising Research Centre (WARC) to empirically identify what types of brand advertising are most effective both for attracting new customers and for converting them into loyal repeaters. As we'll explain, the key to successful brand building is a clear and specific promise to the customer that can be demonstrably fulfilled. Advertising that makes such a promise almost always results in better performance than advertising that does not—even if the latter creates greater name awareness. And a well-designed customer promise not only leads directly to sales but also provides an effective framework on which to organize a company's activities.

Let's begin by explaining what we mean by a "promise to the customer."

Promises, Promises . . .

When one person makes a promise to another, it creates a relationship between the two. If the pledge is fulfilled, it builds trust, resulting in a valuable connection. Research shows conclusively

Idea in Brief

The Problem
The proponents of advertising have always struggled to prove that the money is well spent, making it easy for executives to justify cutting ad budgets.

Why It Happens
The advent of online advertising and "performance marketing," in which the advertiser essentially pays for clicks, has intensified the struggle. That's because in what is now called "brand advertising," the link between ad spending and positive financial outcomes is more tenuous.

The Solution
New research shows that brand-building campaigns anchored in a memorable, valuable, and deliverable promise to the customer are likelier than campaigns that don't make such a promise to result in positive financial performance.

that making a promise and then delivering on it has a greater positive impact on the recipient than simply doing a favor or a service for that person.[1]

Consider these three promises from competitors in the same industry: Allstate's "You're in good hands," "Nationwide is on your side," and Geico's "15 minutes could save you 15%." Only Geico's is direct and verifiable. It promises that just 15 minutes of your time can save you 15% over your current insurance. That creates a connection. And if you take the 15 minutes and save 15% (or more), the company has built trust. Allstate and Nationwide imply promises—but essentially about themselves rather than the customer: Our hands are good hands, and we are on your side. Their promises aren't verifiable. What does "good" mean in practice? And how does "on your side" play out?

Those differences made us wonder: Could a brand-building campaign's success be related to the type of promise it made?

Would customers respond more favorably to a brand that made and then clearly delivered on a specific promise? To answer those questions, we turned to WARC (a sibling of Cannes Lions, which organizes the International Festival of Creativity). WARC's database includes more than 24,000 case studies, drawn from ad competitions all around the world. The competitions require entrants to explain how their marketing communications have worked—including soft performance metrics, such as impact on brand perception, and hard measures, such as gain in market share.

We studied the data for more than 2,000 campaigns that had entered competitions from 2018 to 2022. Before looking at any of the performance metrics, we classified the campaigns according to whether they had made an explicit and verifiable promise to customers. About 60% (1,213 of 2,021) included no such promise, while the remainder (808) did.

We then compared the two groups on a variety of metrics. Customer promise (CP) campaigns outperformed other campaigns across most measures. For example, on measures of brand perception, brand preference, and purchase intent, 56% of CP campaigns—versus 38% of others—reported improvement. Market penetration increased in 45% of CP campaigns versus 38% of other campaigns, and market share increased in 27% of CP campaigns versus 17% of others. That is not to say that other campaigns didn't perform well on some measures. They beat CP campaigns soundly (55% to 43%) on generation of social media buzz, for example.

But CP campaigns win on the important metrics. WARC ranks campaigns in a hierarchy of six ascending levels of performance. Unsuccessful campaigns don't make it into the hierarchy. Non-CP campaigns outperform CP campaigns slightly (51% to 49%) on the lowest level: "influential idea." But as the categories become more important, the advantage of CP over non-CP

The power of a customer promise

Ad campaigns rooted in making and fulfilling a customer promise may not always generate the most buzz, but they deliver on the dimensions that count. The World Advertising Research Centre uses six levels of performance to rate campaigns, shown here from least to most commercially successful. We studied WARC's data for more than 2,000 campaigns to compare their results.

Performance level	Criterion	Does the campaign make a promise to the consumer?	
Influential idea	Overachieves on campaign metrics	No 51%	
		Yes 49	
Behavior breakthrough	Changes consumer behavior	43	
			57
Sales spike	Leads to short-term growth	45	
			55
Brand builder	Improves brand health	41	
			59
Commercial triumph	Creates sustained sales success	38	
			62
Enduring icon	Results in long-term brand and sales growth	33	
			67

Source: World Advertising Research Centre.

campaigns grows, with 62% over 38% in "commercial triumph" and 67% over 33% in "enduring icon."

What Does a Customer Promise Involve?

We began by looking at the kinds of promises made in our dataset of 808 CP campaigns. The majority of promises fell into three types, and 89% of campaigns made at least one type. Some made more than one.

Emotional

Perhaps surprisingly, this was the biggest category, with 35% of the campaigns having made it their primary kind. It involves the emotional benefits a customer will receive from using a product or service. A classic example is the Mastercard "priceless" campaign: "There are some things money can't buy. For everything else, there's Mastercard." The promise is that Mastercard will take care of everything involving money, allowing you to focus on your treasured experiences. Another classic is "Have a Coke and a smile," which focused customers on the pleasure associated with drinking a Coke with someone else. And De Beers's famous "A diamond is forever" has since 1947 promised that the endurance of a diamond confers permanence on the emotions attached to it. More recently Lysol's "Protect Like a Mother" makes the emotional promise that using the product will make you as protective as fierce mothers in the animal kingdom.

Functional

In 32% of our sample the primary promise was functional. For instance, Snickers's "You're not you when you're hungry" promises that customers will be able to operate at full capacity after consuming one of its candy bars. FedEx launched its "When it absolutely, positively has to be there overnight" campaign in 1978, and the promise was so powerful that it resulted in the creation of a new verb: to FedEx. Part of the campaign's success is that it conveys an emotional promise as well: You don't have to worry, because it's FedEx.

Enjoyable to buy

A surprisingly large number of companies (22%) adopted as their primary promise the idea that customers would enjoy the process of purchasing. A good example is provided by the paint maker Sherwin-Williams, which won the 2022 B2B Grand Prix at Cannes for its campaign based on an artificial intelligence tool that allows customers to create and choose a paint color by using voice to describe it ("a turquoise like the sea in the Maldives," for example). Designers and architects loved it. The promise that Uber is "the smartest way to get around," which focuses heavily on the ease of ordering and paying, is another example.

The remaining campaigns fell into three minor categories: *value for money* (5%), such as Geico's "15 minutes could save you 15%"; *sustainability* (4%), including Tide's "Turn to Cold" campaign, which promises that its new product is as effective in cold water as regular Tide is in hot; and *making amends* for prior failures (2%), with Wells Fargo's "Earning back your trust" campaign in the wake of its fraudulent account-opening scandal being a prime example.

Having determined what kinds of promises companies make, we turned to look at what makes the promises attractive to customers. We found that successful campaigns share three features. They are:

Memorable

In most cases they run counter to expectations. Germany-based SIXT has quickly become the fourth-largest rental car company in Europe and is the fastest growing in the U.S. market. Its slogan is "Don't Rent a Car, Rent *the* Car." Its promise is that SIXT won't disappoint you by foisting the only available vehicle on you when you arrive for pickup, as often happens to customers at other companies. You'll be given the car you originally chose.

Valuable

Customers must want what the promise offers. That's more likely if it diverges from a status quo they don't like. SIXT executives realized that customers willing to hire an expensive car actually cared about the make and model. That was less of an issue for bargain hunters—but they weren't SIXT's target market. Of course, other rental companies also offer premium cars, but in order to save costs, they don't always guarantee a specific car, giving SIXT an opportunity to differentiate itself with premium buyers.

Deliverable

Part of the value of any customer promise is precisely that it is a guarantee, which requires that the customer be able to determine that the promise was fulfilled. Making a promise involves risks. SIXT must deliver *the* car. Mastercard actually needs to take care of "everything else." Coke has to be enjoyable (which is why its reputation suffered so much when people didn't like the taste of New Coke); Lysol must protect; Snickers must boost energy, and so on. Our assumption is that most of the 808 CP campaigns generally fulfilled their companies' promises; otherwise, they wouldn't have had disproportionally positive effects. But because customer promise has not been an explicit factor in previous surveys, the WARC dataset includes no information about whether the companies making such promises actually fulfilled them. Our hypothesis is that had we been able to create a subsample of campaigns that definitively made good on their promises, we would have found that they scored even higher on the performance metrics. Of course, how a customer determines whether the promise has been kept may not be obvious, especially in emotional-value campaigns. But it clearly makes sense for companies to figure out exactly how to deliver on their promises.

Marketers always claim that their goal is to make campaign promises memorable, valuable, and deliverable. But as we've seen, their promises aren't always about the customer. The premier advertising event of the year is the Super Bowl, when many viewers pay more attention to the ads than to the game, and the 2023 Super Bowl was no exception. Most of the ads were feats of creative storytelling packed into a precious few seconds of very expensive airtime. They were memorable and often featured celebrities: the Hellman's mayonnaise ad depicted *Brie* Larson and Jon *Hamm* about to be eaten in a sandwich by Pete Davidson.

But our appraisal of the 51 commercials for the 2023 Super Bowl reveals that fewer than a third of them attempted to convey a specific promise of value to be delivered to the customer—a finding close to our results when we broke down the WARC campaigns. What most of those ads were aiming at was to enter the cultural conversation—advertising's equivalent of trying to be the most popular kid at the party. Only a handful actually made their tagline a memorable, valuable, and deliverable promise to the customer. Farmer's Dog, which promised "Real Food. Made Fresh. Delivered," was one.

We don't have the data to assert that its Super Bowl ad boosted sales for Farmer's Dog more than the other ads did for their companies. But feedback we got on our research suggests that it's very likely. When we showed our results to one major advertiser, for example, its executives decided to review the copy of three successive ad campaigns: a successful one followed by a disappointing one followed by a successful one. Everyone in the room agreed that the company had made an explicit promise in the first and the third, but its executives had been so excited about a new version of the product featured in the second that they had focused the ad on how great it was and neglected to make a promise.

The insight that effective brand building is anchored in a promise to the customer can do more for a company than just help it invest wisely in advertising. The promise can serve as a strategic framework for mobilizing everything a company does.

Your Promise Is Your Strategy

Today's companies face big challenges stemming from the fragmentation of functions including product, marketing, sales, customer experience and loyalty, and HR and talent. They all tend to operate in silos, often at significant cross-purposes.

A well-conceived customer promise can provide a common objective. That's because creating and executing on a CP is, in essence, an act of strategy making—defining where the company will play (for SIXT, among affluent people who care about cars) and how it will win (by guaranteeing they get the car they chose). This provides information for investors (how the company will beat its competitors), customers (the value the company will bring them), employees (the value they are striving to create), the marketing and sales function (how the company positions itself), the production function (what the operational objective is), and finance (what it should be measuring).

We think of taking a CP to the market as a cycle with five steps. The first step is to *understand* customers well enough to know what constitutes memorability and value for them. SIXT understood its customers well enough to know that they were frustrated by being given a rental car they hadn't chosen and didn't like. It used that understanding to *design* a CP, settling on a very simple but compelling and memorable statement: "Don't Rent a Car, Rent *the* Car." The first half of the tagline is counterintuitive—*No, I need a rental car!*—but the second half makes a specific and deliverable promise: *SIXT said I would be given the car I booked—and I was.* Once a company has designed its CP, it can *issue* it publicly and, in doing so, commit to it, which SIXT does relentlessly. Then it must *project* that promise to the target audience: if it isn't received, it can't be effective. Finally, it needs to *fulfill* the CP, or the promise will be largely worthless. SIXT unfailingly does so.

This cycle provides guidance about the resources the company must dedicate to the various aspects of brand building. How much should it dedicate to understanding customers? How much to designing and issuing a CP? How much to projecting it? And how much to ensuring that the key aspects of the CP are delivered? As the company repeats the cycle, it learns more about its strategic challenges and how to account for customer and competitor shifts.

The ultimate goal of a marketing campaign should be to go through the CP cycle often enough that your customers stop wondering whether you'll make good on your promises. Once they assume that you will, they purchase out of habit rather than choice. Tide customers don't question whether the detergent will get their clothes whiter and brighter. They just dump it in the shopping cart. This unthinking habit means that they give Tide's competitors no opportunity to prove their own CPs, widening Tide's lead over the competition. The result is an enduring and valuable brand.

So when a CMO comes to the excom meeting to propose allocating capital to a new campaign, the CEO and the CFO should ask four simple questions: (1) Is the campaign based on a clear and unambiguous customer promise? (2) Were customer insights used to identify a promise that customers value? (3) Is the promise framed in a way that is truly memorable? (4) Were product, marketing, sales, and customer experience involved to ensure that it will be consistently fulfilled?

If any of the answers are negative, the CMO needs to go back to the drawing board. But if they're all positive, the company should absolutely invest in the campaign, because those questions capture the secret to brand building.

Originally published in January–February 2024. Reprint R2401K

10

Is Your Marketing Organization Ready for What's Next?

by Omar Rodríguez-Vilá, Sundar Bharadwaj, Neil A. Morgan, and Shubu Mitra

arketing has never been more complex. Sweeping advances in technology have revolutionized and fragmented the discipline, while societal issues such as the Covid-19 pandemic, the Black Lives Matter movement, and the climate crisis have raised expectations for marketers' social performance. This combination of diverse forces has transformed how the marketing function must work, requiring that it become more agile, interdependent, and accountable for driving company growth.

It's no wonder that leaders are uncertain about marketing's role and anxious about its performance. Our survey of marketing managers at 493 companies found that just 20% of those in traditional corporations are satisfied with the effectiveness of their departments; the percentage is only marginally higher among those in digital-native companies. With the support of the Mobile Marketing Association and in collaboration with Peter Schelstraete, formerly the global vice president of digital and assets at Coca-Cola, we spent two years studying the change in marketing organizations. We conducted in-depth interviews with 125 senior marketing leaders across industries to understand the problem and to learn how they were adapting their organizations to compete in this new environment. Most of them, we found, strategically invested in marketing activities, technologies, and structures in order to capitalize on new growth opportunities.

Yet many of their efforts to transform marketing organizations were complicated by the lack of a structured methodology. To create a practical framework that companies could use, we started by identifying the ways in which a marketing function can contribute to company growth. That led us to define six broad areas of value. We then developed an inventory of 72 marketing capabilities, spanning both new and foundational tasks, that are needed to create that value. To our knowledge, this is the most comprehensive compendium of its kind. With input from a steering committee composed of 10 chief marketing officers of leading companies, we then created the analytic process presented here. It can be used to define a marketing value proposition, select the necessary capabilities, and design a competitive next-generation function. Our model has now guided marketing transformations at digital-native and traditional companies across industries, including consumer packaged goods, transportation, financial services, and retail.

Idea in Brief

The Problem

Leaders are finding it difficult to think clearly about the role of the marketing function and are anxious about its performance. Yet their efforts to transform marketing have at times been stymied by the lack of a clear methodology for defining its job and designing its work.

The Framework

The authors offer a practical framework for clarifying how marketing can contribute to company growth by delivering distinctive types of value to customers and to the organization itself.

The Result

Companies across industries have applied this framework to reveal the gap between their existing and needed areas of focus; to determine which capabilities to develop, which to sustain at their current level, and which to scale down, outsource, or automate; and to redesign their marketing functions to deliver on a new value proposition.

Defining Marketing's Value Proposition

We found that marketing leaders struggle with transformation efforts for three key reasons. First, they often look at the transformation as an exercise in retooling technology or reshaping structures rather than rethinking how a changing environment can enable the function to create new types of value. Second, they commonly frame transformation projects as a transition from one state to another—for example, from brand to performance marketing or, simply, old to new. That mindset can inhibit synergies between traditional and current marketing practices, splinter teams, and distract from a focus on customers. Third, leaders often allow modernization efforts to be dispersed across teams or functional areas without a holistic operating framework. As a result, various groups may be pursuing distinct and uncoordinated change initiatives, fragmenting value-creation efforts, and undermining marketing's ability to drive growth.

Without a clear, value-based goal for marketing and a strategy for determining the capabilities needed to achieve it, new technologies, structures, and processes are unlikely to deliver substantial improvements in performance. Our framework provides both the goal and the strategy. It divides the six kinds of value created into two categories: value for customers and value for the company. Understanding this taxonomy is the first step in articulating your marketing value proposition and the starting point for aligning marketing's activities with the company's growth strategy.

Creating Customer Value

In the effort to attract, acquire, and retain customers, a marketing team can create value for them in three areas: *exchange*, *experience*, and *engagement*.

Exchange value

Marketers create this kind of value when they effectively match their offerings to specific customer needs. That requires recognizing when customers are looking for a particular product or service, understanding what problem they are trying to solve, and figuring out what offerings will suit them best—in real time. It calls for sharp *conversion*, *personalization*, and *prediction* capabilities.

To maximize exchange value, marketers use sophisticated analytics and machine learning to process vast amounts of data on consumer behavior. Allstate, for example, targets dozens of customer types with hundreds of products and tailored messages developed through the use of AI. Alibaba draws on real-time data and continuously fine-tuned learning algorithms to deliver personalized offers to millions of customers. MTailor uses an AI-powered app to measure customers' fit and deliver customized clothing, and Stitch Fix depends on machine learning to help personalize wardrobe recommendations.

The exchange-value-focused CMOs in our study embrace computer science and are emphatic about the importance of AI in shaping the marketing discipline. As one of them put it, "If you can't have a conversation about pixels or attribution models, you are stuck in the past."

Experience value

Marketers focused on creating this kind of value work to eliminate hassles and enhance satisfaction across the customer journey. That requires a focus on improving *journey orchestration*, *value augmentation*, and *offering design* through constant innovation.

Delta Air Lines, for instance, has become a master at anticipating travelers' needs and addressing them with customized messages. The airline enhances its core product—the flight—by smoothing the service experience around it, providing advice and information on traffic to and from the airport, in-flight dining choices, boarding status, baggage location, and more. Such service proficiency across the customer journey improves both customer satisfaction and loyalty.

Some companies are creating new types of experience value in China by innovatively integrating mobile technology and delivery infrastructures. For example, KFC's Shanghai stores accept orders via mobile apps and deliver food to long-distance train passengers at their stop of choice.

Value for the customer

Marketing creates customer value in three areas: engagement, experience, and exchange. Comparing the function's current capabilities within each area with those it will need to effectively compete in the future reveals gaps in preparedness. The analysis shown here exposes significant deficits in story design, personalization, and prediction capabilities.

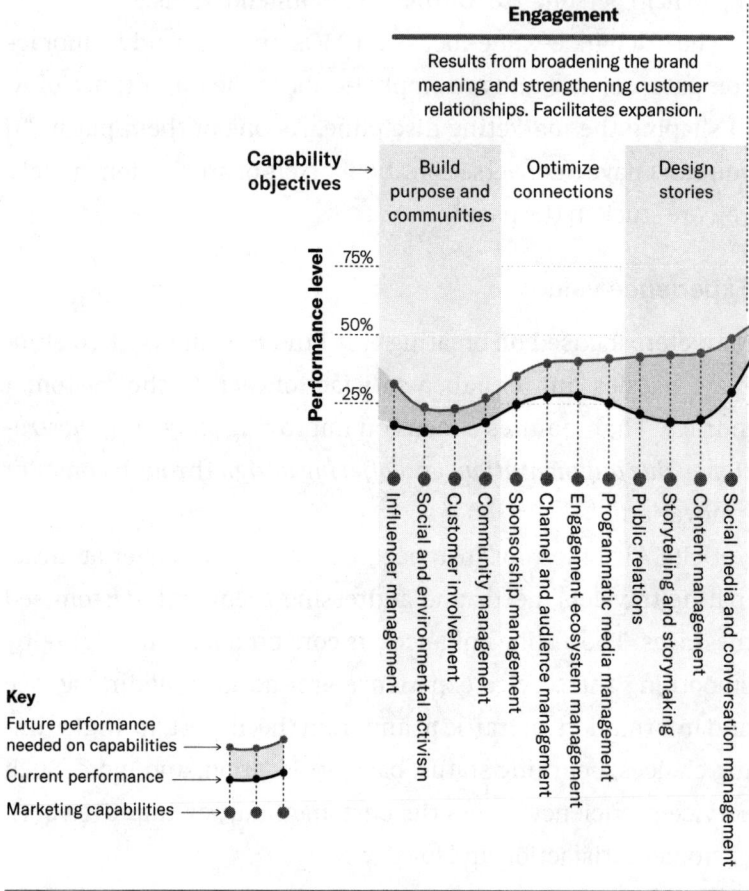

Engagement

Results from broadening the brand meaning and strengthening customer relationships. Facilitates expansion.

Capability objectives →

| Build purpose and communities | Optimize connections | Design stories |

Performance level: 75%, 50%, 25%

Influencer management
Social and environmental activism
Customer involvement
Community management
Sponsorship management
Channel and audience management
Engagement ecosystem management
Programmatic media management
Public relations
Storytelling and storymaking
Content management
Social media and conversation management

Key

Future performance needed on capabilities →

Current performance →

Marketing capabilities →

Experience

Results from increasing convenience and enjoyment across the customer journey. Facilitates retention.

Exchange

Results from matching offerings to individual customer needs and context. Facilitates transactions.

| Augment value | Improve journey orchestration | Enhance offering design | Boost conversion | Increase personalization | Improve prediction |

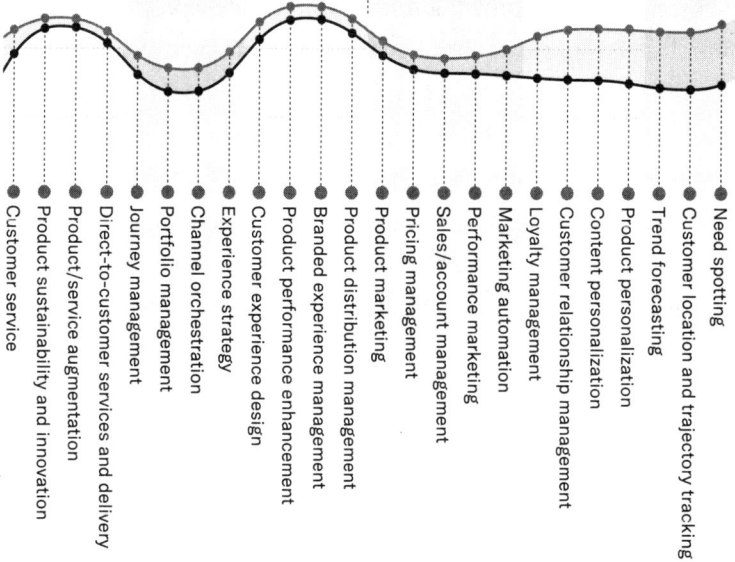

- Customer service
- Product sustainability and innovation
- Product/service augmentation
- Direct-to-customer services and delivery
- Journey management
- Portfolio management
- Channel orchestration
- Experience strategy
- Customer experience design
- Product performance enhancement
- Branded experience management
- Product distribution management
- Product marketing
- Pricing management
- Sales/account management
- Performance marketing
- Marketing automation
- Loyalty management
- Customer relationship management
- Content personalization
- Product personalization
- Trend forecasting
- Customer location and trajectory tracking
- Need spotting

Engagement value

This type of value enhances the "meaning" of a company's offering—how customers perceive the brand and their relationship with it. Companies increasingly create it by merging traditional techniques such as storytelling and public relations with dynamic content-management systems that facilitate and sometimes automate the design and delivery of real-time messages. They also nurture a sense of community among users and go beyond a product's traditional functional or emotional benefits to offer societal benefits—for example, by adopting an environmental or social mission. Creating engagement value requires marketers to *build purpose and communities, optimize connections,* and *design stories* to strengthen customer relationships.

Brands across sectors have embraced social activism in authentic ways: REI, with its focus on environmental stewardship; Always, with its commitment to strengthening self-esteem among young women; and Danone, as a champion of more-sustainable food, to name just a few. All these brands have nurtured active customer involvement with their social efforts. Their work has reinforced meaning, relevance, and trust and led to levels of engagement that would have been difficult to achieve through product-centered efforts alone.

Marketers can also increase engagement value by encouraging customers to interact with one another, asking questions, sharing knowledge, and collaborating. To this end, Salesforce created the Trailblazer Community, where customers can join dozens of user groups across industries to share their experiences with the company's products. Similarly, Glossier, a direct-to-consumer beauty-products brand, facilitates community groups focused on pertinent topics. User groups help these companies understand customer needs, enhance retention, lower acquisition costs, generate product ideas, and smooth the introduction of innovations. For instance, Glossier is exploring social commerce that involves community members who act as influencers and even sell its products.

Creating Company Value

The marketing function can also contribute to growth by generating internal value for a company in three areas: *strategic, operational,* and *knowledge.*

Strategic value

Marketing teams often spot ways to expand current offerings and guide the development of new offerings and business models. To do this they need the ability to *discover growth, build platforms,* and *leverage assets.* Traditionally they focused to a large extent on identifying opportunities for line extensions within a given product category. Today technology allows marketers to help companies enter new categories and even industries as never before. Consider Google's move into autonomous vehicles. The company has continually expanded its capabilities and brand meaning, enabling it to compete in businesses that its former sector rival Yahoo would be hard-pressed to try. The energy drink Red Bull has likewise broken through category boundaries, creating the successful sports and lifestyle platform Red Bull Media House.

Marketing teams can also help companies capture new revenue streams from existing assets or practices—for example, by monetizing marketing data and activities. Amazon's advertising unit has reported revenue of $10 billion from product sponsorships, placements, the creation of brand-specific stores, and other efforts. Target has created a new revenue stream with Roundel, its recently rebranded media network, which develops content and campaigns for its brand and agency clients, using its own customer data. Caterpillar has placed sensors in more than a million products to generate utilization data services that help large construction and mining companies optimize the maintenance and use of their equipment.

Marketing leaders can also play a central role in creating or identifying new business models and technologies that spur customer demand. For example, many large companies—Unilever among them—have established units to manage investments in startups and new ventures in emerging marketing technology or entertainment services that, among other things, can help shape product, service, or marketing efforts.

Operational value

Marketing's role in strengthening a company's operating effectiveness has never been more important. Yet many marketing leaders struggle with the proliferation of independent and specialized teams engaged in an expanding array of activities across the organization. Because these teams often have divergent methods and views about the role of marketing and its contribution to growth, their work can be hard to integrate. As one of the executives in our study explained, "No technology in the world, no digital marketing, no attribution model, can overcome a lack of alignment across an organization. If one team is measuring success one way and another team is measuring success another way—good luck making it work." The key here is the ability to *improve talent management, enhance organizational links,* and *strengthen execution methods and technology.*

Marketing organizations create operational value for a company by aligning disparate teams around a shared growth agenda and marketing approach and increasing their speed, agility, and collaboration. In part that requires constantly upgrading marketing technologies to automate and integrate many aspects of customer relationship management at scale and in real time. We saw three strategies for achieving this.

First, effective CMOs establish a clear set of marketing principles and methods—a blueprint for getting the function's work done. It includes developing shared language and frameworks, understanding how relevant key performance indicators are connected, and creating common accounting standards and flexible decision processes.

Second, they foster an organizational culture that focuses on customer needs and more-fluid interactions between areas of expertise. One tool we saw put to that purpose was "key behavioral indicators" (KBIs), such as levels of interpersonal trust and transparency, which were accorded the same status as KPIs in performance evaluations. That's because when performance on KBIs falls, one CMO told us, the time needed for alignment and coordination increases, reducing speed to market.

Third, these CMOs adopt technologies that help reduce the costs of coordination and collaboration and increase efficiency, transparency, and trust by enabling interaction across teams. Those technologies include project management applications such as Slack, communication platforms, knowledge management systems, and live meeting webcasts to promote inclusion.

Value for the company

Marketing creates company value in three areas: knowledge, strategic, and operational. Comparing the function's current capabilities within each area with those it will need to effectively compete in the future reveals gaps in preparedness. The analysis shown here exposes significant deficits across all three, most notably in building platforms.

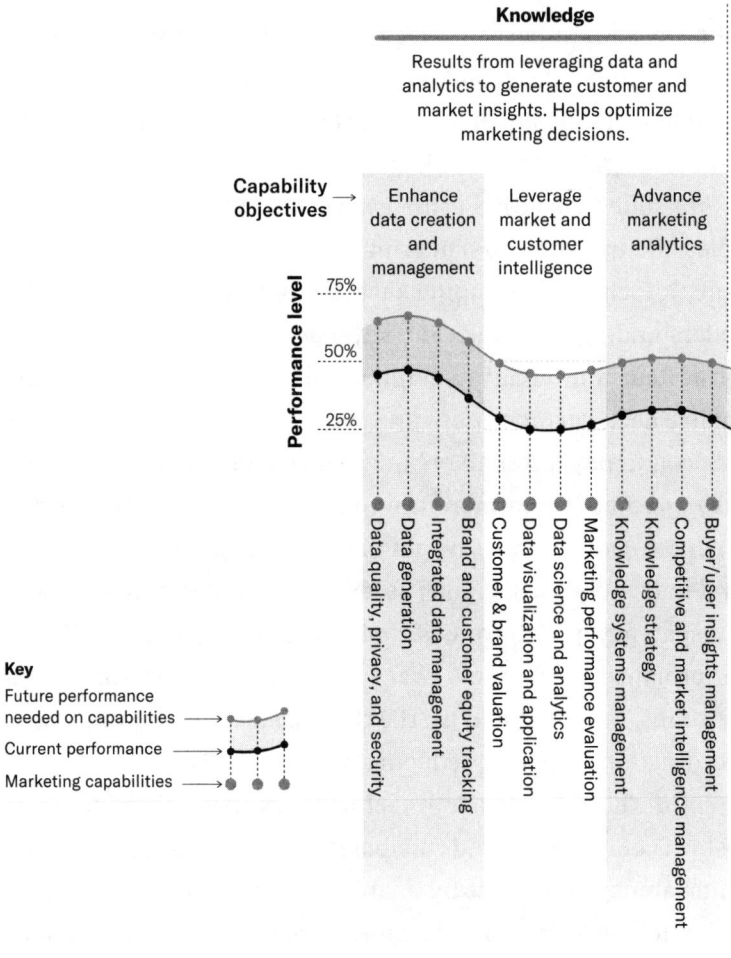

Knowledge

Results from leveraging data and analytics to generate customer and market insights. Helps optimize marketing decisions.

Capability objectives →

Enhance data creation and management

Leverage market and customer intelligence

Advance marketing analytics

Performance level — 75%, 50%, 25%

Marketing capabilities: Data quality, privacy, and security; Data generation; Integrated data management; Brand and customer equity tracking; Customer & brand valuation; Data visualization and application; Data science and analytics; Marketing performance evaluation; Knowledge systems management; Knowledge strategy; Competitive and market intelligence management; Buyer/user insights management

Key

Future performance needed on capabilities →

Current performance →

Marketing capabilities →

Strategic			Operational		
Results from identifying growth opportunities that can be connected to current offerings. Helps develop new offerings and business models.			Results from improving organizational agility, collaboration, and talent development. Helps strengthen operating effectiveness.		
Discover growth	Build platforms	Leverage assets	Improve talent management	Enhance organizational links	Strengthen execution methods and technology

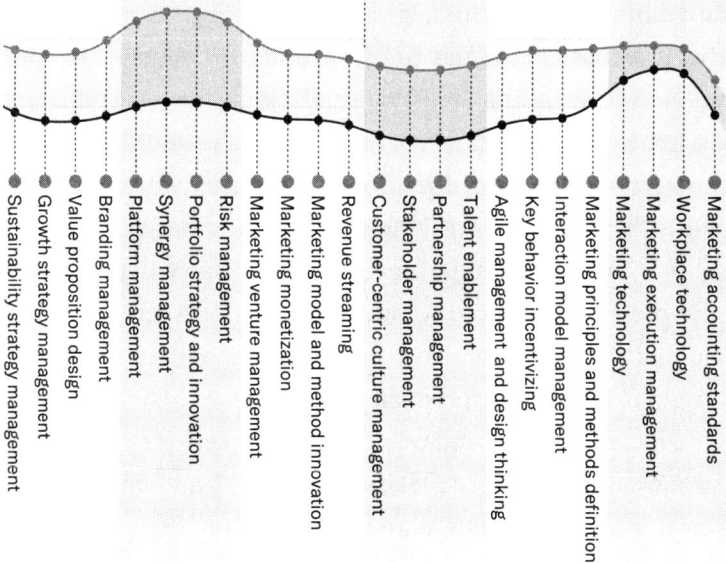

Sustainability strategy management
Growth strategy management
Value proposition design
Branding management
Platform management
Synergy management
Portfolio strategy and innovation
Risk management
Marketing venture management
Marketing monetization
Marketing model and method innovation
Revenue streaming
Customer-centric culture management
Stakeholder management
Partnership management
Talent enablement
Agile management and design thinking
Key behavior incentivizing
Interaction model management
Marketing principles and methods definition
Marketing technology
Marketing execution management
Workplace technology
Marketing accounting standards

Knowledge value

In its role representing the "voice of the customer," the marketing function can create knowledge value, principally through the astute use of data science. Some established customer-intelligence activities, such as user-needs assessments and sentiment tracking, remain important. But newer technologies open up further opportunities. For example, AI-powered data analytics systems can increasingly tease out the causal relationship between marketing investments and business outcomes, improving marketing efficiency. The success of such initiatives depends on *enhancing data creation and management, leveraging market and customer intelligence,* and *advancing marketing analytics.*

In addition, new technologies are enabling ever more innovative ways for companies to capture market signals and use data. For instance, the Freestyle vending machine installed by Coca-Cola across thousands of quick-service restaurants allows customers to select from dozens of flavor mixes, which are individually dispensed. By tracking and reporting these orders, the machines provide granular, real-time, first-party data on consumer preferences: a highly valuable asset for a non-direct-to-consumer firm. The company has used this data to inform its R&D and to launch new products.

As a major producer and user of data, marketing can also create knowledge value by collaborating with IT and data science teams to generate a single source of market intelligence, devise ways to define and measure key marketing metrics, and develop mechanisms for protecting customer information. Adobe executives credit the creation of such a "single source of truth" as a key turning point in accelerating the company's transformation effort.

Determine Your Marketing Value Proposition

With a clear understanding of these six broad types of value and the capabilities needed to deliver them, leaders can gauge the importance of each to future growth. That analysis will yield the function's value proposition—its statement of purpose.

Using our framework, a team of marketing leaders and other executives can engage in a series of sessions in which they systematically rate the importance to growth over the coming two or three years of each of the 72 capabilities underpinning the six value areas. For example, they can ask, Within exchange value, how important to growth on a 1 (low) to 10 (high) scale will trend forecasting be? Product personalization? Marketing automation? And so on.

The team can use a discrete-choice method such as conjoint analysis or MaxDiff to analyze data from various stakeholders in determining the relative importance of the types of value. This step helps leaders think clearly about the difference between the value that marketing currently creates and what it *should* create according to its potential to drive sales, profits, and company growth. For instance, our analyses across 10 industries show that technology-enabled convenience benefits are more important to buyers of services than to buyers of products. In contrast, purpose-related benefits, such as a brand's stance on social issues, are more important to buyers of consumer packaged goods than to buyers of services.

During this exercise it is important to be clear about what's feasible. We have seen no company become "best in class" in all six areas simultaneously; instead each organization makes careful choices about what it will focus on given its growth goals, industry conditions, competitive environment, and other factors that

---

A Digital Scoring Tool

The scoring exercise we describe here can be done manually. For a quick introduction to our analytic process, readers can take a simplified version of the online assessment created by our firm, MarCaps, which provides a general score for the fit between a company's current and necessary marketing capabilities, and benchmarks the organization against others that have used the tool. The assessment is available at https://www.marcaps.com/about-3.

---

affect strategy. All companies have constraints related to finances, data availability, and their marketing function's heritage. The key in refining the marketing value proposition is to determine which subset of value areas marketing can best develop, given its resources and constraints.

Assess Your Fit

This exercise reveals where the greatest opportunity to create value lies and what specific capabilities will be needed to realize it. The team can gauge marketing's readiness to deliver by scoring its *current* performance on each of the 72 capabilities. (See the sidebar "A Digital Scoring Tool" for how to access a simplified version of our assessment.) When those scores are plotted on a chart, gaps between current capabilities and future needs reveal where the organization should act.

This analysis won't yield a mandate for specific change. Rather, it will provide a road map showing a variety of paths that leaders can follow, taking into account the company's priorities and capabilities. Typically, companies select a subset of areas for investment, considering both the fit level revealed by the analysis and the efforts that will be required to address those areas.

Create Your Change Strategy

Once marketing's areas of strength and weakness have been identified, it's clearer which capabilities to develop, which to sustain at their current level, and which to scale down, outsource, or automate. But it's usually easier for leaders to launch new initiatives or even maintain the status quo than to pull resources from existing activities. In our conversations with CMOs, many talked about the challenge, and the importance, of deciding what *not* to do, particularly in large organizations where resources and an appetite for exploration may be substantial.

Consider how the chief marketing officer of a leading transportation technology firm we worked with applied the framework. She formed a marketing transformation team that included the marketing directors of each geographic region, members of the global marketing organization, and representatives from human resources. In a series of work sessions over six weeks, the team rated the importance to company growth of capabilities within each area and aligned around a value proposition that focused on increasing exchange, engagement, operational, and knowledge value.

We then worked with the team to evaluate the current level of each capability and the level needed to help deliver on the new value proposition. In a final work session, the leaders made specific choices about their organizational priorities for the following year and where they needed to invest to achieve them. This process underscores the assessment's role as a form of guidance rather than a strict mandate. Although the analysis revealed opportunities for improvement in each of the value categories the team selected, the group decided not to invest substantially at that time in enhancing strategic value. The CMO and her team clearly saw an opportunity to create that kind of value by finding new sources of revenue, but various organizational constraints suggested that they could reap a higher ROI on their investments in capability building elsewhere.

The priorities they selected included prediction and conversion management, storytelling and content personalization, market and customer intelligence, talent enablement, organizational links, data science and analytics, and marketing technology. This new focus led to the formation of the company's first marketing operations and capability functions, the formalization of a branding team, and the integration of its product and performance marketing activities into the team focused on demand generation. Just as important, the work created a clarity of purpose that provided unified and much-needed direction to the company's marketing staff.

As the CMO put it, "It helped us get aligned within our team and with the executive team on what we needed to be best in the world at, what we needed to be good at, and what we could assign to others."

. . .

Marketing leaders have recognized and acted on the need to change their organizations. But most have struggled to carry out changes in ways that advance marketing's operating effectiveness. The framework presented here brings clarity to the process and guides the design of a marketing organization for our time—one built as a coalition to create value and drive company growth.

Originally published in November–December 2020. Reprint R2006H

Discussion Guide

Are you feeling inspired by what you've read in this collection? Do you want to share the ideas in the articles or explore the insights you've gleaned with others? This discussion guide offers an opportunity to dig a little deeper, with questions to prompt personal reflection and to start conversations with your team.

You don't need to have read the book from beginning to end to use this guide. Choose the questions that apply to the articles you have read or that you feel might spark the liveliest discussion.

Reflect on key takeaways from your reading to help you adopt the ideas and techniques you want to integrate into your work as a leader. What tools can you share with your team to help everyone be their best? Becoming the leader you want to be starts with a detailed plan—and a commitment to carrying it out.

1. Why do your customers choose your company over your competitors' companies, and what needs do you fulfill for your customers? Who are your current competitors? What other threats and substitutes could disrupt your business if you look beyond direct rivals?

2. What are the advantages and disadvantages of using Net Promoter Score to assess customer satisfaction in your business? What investments do you need to make to increase visibility into customer loyalty and tie it to financial outcomes?

3. How are you balancing human and machine-led decisions in your marketing efforts? What key decision points would benefit from relying on intuition, and where does it make sense to be more data-driven? How can you develop the right mindset and capabilities on your team so that everyone can switch nimbly and effectively between approaches and make the most of humans' *and* AI's talents?

4. In the article, "Personalization Done Right," Mark Abraham and David C. Edelman present the "five promises of personalization": *empower me, know me, reach me, show me,* and *delight me.* In which of these areas is your company strong, and where can you improve to better meet customers' needs? In what ways could you be taking greater advantage of AI to create more personalization?

5. What are your impressions of psychological targeting, both as a consumer and as a marketer? For companies that use this technique, what ethical guardrails need to be in place to ensure fairness, privacy, transparency, and consent? What are some issues and pain points that tailored interventions could help you solve for your customers?

6. How would you define the role and expectations of the CMO in your organization? What could be done to improve the CMO's cross-functional partnerships, especially with the CIO? What lessons can be learned from past hiring processes or known CMO failures of fit in your industry?

7. Describe an instance in which sales' and marketing's goals diverged and how the differences were handled. What could have been done to synchronize efforts more? How

can you ensure better alignment in the future, and what metrics can be put in place to measure it?

8. In what areas of brand management is human judgment indispensable—and where can AI assist? What other companies are capturing value from AI in their branding, and what makes these applications so powerful? What inspiration can you draw from their examples for your own business?

9. What new audiences or customer segments do you want to reach, and how do they differ from your existing customers? How might you mitigate segment conflict so that you don't alienate one segment of customers by catering to another? Are there opportunities to foster synergies between segments?

10. Have you ever purchased a product after seeing an influencer share it? What drew you in—or deterred you from buying? Think of the seven variables of effective campaigns outlined in "Does Influencer Marketing Really Pay Off?"—when does it make sense for your brand to use an influencer and when should you consider a different approach?

11. Describe your company's customer promise. How would you rate it in terms of being truly memorable, valuable, and deliverable? What would it look like for an ad campaign to compellingly reflect this promise?

12. What is your marketing function's core value proposition? What would it take to deliver sufficient value to both customers and the company? Which capabilities do you

consider organizational strengths and which do you still need to develop to drive growth and deliver on marketing's value proposition?

13. What other sources on marketing have had a significant impact on your work? Were there voices or subtopics you missed in this collection? Were there voices or subtopics included that surprised you?

14. After reading and reflecting on this book and discussing it with people on your team, write down the ideas and techniques you want to try. Think of how you might experiment and implement those in both the short term and the long term. Draft a plan to move forward.

Notes

Chapter 1: Marketing Myopia

1. Jacques Barzun, "Trains and the Mind of Man," *Holiday*, February 1960.
2. For more details, see M. M. Zimmerman, *The Super Market: A Revolution in Distribution* (McGraw-Hill, 1955).
3. Zimmerman, *The Super Market*, pp. 45–47.
4. John Kenneth Galbraith, *The Affluent Society* (Houghton Mifflin, 1958).
5. Henry Ford, *My Life and Work* (Doubleday, 1923).
6. Barzun, "Trains and the Mind of Man."

Quick Read: Are Your Marketing and Sales Teams on the Same Page?

1. Superoffice, "How Sales and Marketing Alignment Increased New Revenue by 34%," November 9, 2023, https://www.superoffice.com/blog/sales-marketing-alignment/.
2. LinkedIn, "Moments of Trust: Why Customer Value Is the Key to Marketing and Sales Alignment," https://business.linkedin.com/content/dam/me/business/en-us/marketing-solutions/cx/2020/images/pdfs/moments-of-trust-v4.pdf.
3. Elizabeth Sullivan-Hasson, "The 2021 B2B Buying Disconnect," November 10, 2020, https://solutions.trustradius.com/vendor-blog/b2b-buying-disconnect-2021/.

Quick Read: Does Influencer Marketing Really Pay Off?

1. Influencer Marketing Hub, "Influencer Marketing Benchmark Report 2025," April 25, 2025, https://influencermarketinghub.com/influencer-marketing-benchmark-report/.
2. Djanan Kasumovic, "10 Examples of Influencer Marketing Campaigns (+Strategic Insights for Brands)," Influencer Marketing Hub, June 18, 2025, https://influencermarketinghub.com/influencer-marketing-examples/.
3. Fine F. Leung, Jonathan Z. Zhang, Flora F. Gu, Yiwei Li, and Robert W. Palmatier, "Influencer Marketing Effectiveness," *Journal of Marketing* 86, no. 6 (2022): 93–115.
4. John Hughes, "5 Powerful Practices for Effective Social Media Linking," Pretty Links, July 18, 2022, https://prettylinks.com/blog/social-media-linking-best-practices/.

Chapter 9: The Right Way to Build Your Brand

1. Daniel Balliet and Paul A. M. Van Lange, "Trust, Punishment, and Cooperation Across 18 Societies: A Meta-Analysis," *Perspectives on Psychological Science* 8, no. 4 (2013), https://doi.org/10.1177/1745691613488533.

About the Contributors

Mark Abraham is a managing director and a senior partner at Boston Consulting Group. He is also the coauthor of *Personalized: Customer Strategy in the Age of AI* (Harvard Business Review Press, 2024).

Sundar Bharadwaj is the Coca-Cola Company Chair of Marketing at the University of Georgia's Terry College of Business. Connect with him on LinkedIn at Sundar Bharadwaj.

Maureen Burns is a senior partner in Bain & Company's Boston office.

Darci Darnell is the head of Bain & Company's customer practice.

Julian De Freitas is an assistant professor of business administration in the marketing unit at Harvard Business School.

David C. Edelman is an executive advisor, a board director, and a fellow at Harvard Business School. He is also the coauthor of *Personalized: Customer Strategy in the Age of AI* (Harvard Business Review Press, 2024).

Fabrizio Fantini is the vice president of product strategy at ToolsGroup and the founder and former CEO of Evo Pricing, a firm offering AI solutions to automate and optimize pricing and supply-chain decisions.

Flora F. Gu is a professor of marketing and the associate head (Knowledge Transfer) at the Department of Management and Marketing, Hong Kong Polytechnic University. Her research interests include marketing strategy, digital marketing, and sales channels.

Ryan Hamilton is an associate professor of marketing at Emory University's Goizueta Business School. He cohosts the podcast *The Intuitive Customer* and has produced a lecture series on marketing and human decision-making for the Great Courses. He is a coauthor of *The Growth Dilemma* (Harvard Business Review Press, 2025).

Fine F. Leung is an associate professor of marketing in the Department of Management and Marketing, Hong Kong Polytechnic University. Her research interests include marketing strategy, influencer marketing, and customer relationship management.

Theodore Levitt was a professor emeritus of marketing at Harvard Business School and former editor of *Harvard Business Review*.

Yiwei Li is an associate professor in the Department of Marketing and International Business at Lingnan University.

Roger L. Martin is a former dean of the Rotman School of Management, an advisor to CEOs, and the author of *A New Way to Think* (Harvard Business Review Press, 2022).

Sandra Matz is the Lulu Chow Wang Professor of Business at Columbia Business School and the author of *Mindmasters* (Harvard Business Review Press, 2025). As a computational social scientist with a background in psychology and computer science, she studies human behavior by uncovering the hidden relationships between our digital lives and our psychology.

Shubu Mitra is a founder and the COO of MarCaps, a marketing capability solutions provider. Connect with him on LinkedIn at Shubu Mitra.

Neil A. Morgan is the Welch Family Professor of Marketing at the Wisconsin School of Business and a founder of MarCaps, a marketing capability solutions provider. Connect with him on LinkedIn at Neil A. Morgan.

Das Narayandas is the Edsel Bryant Ford Professor of Business Administration at Harvard Business School.

Elie Ofek is the Malcolm P. McNair Professor of Marketing at Harvard Business School.

Robert W. Palmatier is a professor of marketing and the John C. Narver Endowed Professor of Business Administration at the Foster School of Business at the University of Washington, where he founded and serves as the research director of the Center for Sales and Marketing Strategy. His research has appeared in multiple academic journals and in *Nature, The Economist, The New York Times Magazine,* and the *Los Angeles Times.*

Kelsey Raymond is the executive director for Entrepreneurship Programs at the University of Missouri-Columbia. She previously served as COO of Intero Digital and president of Intero Digital's Content & PR Division (formerly Influence & Co). Intero Digital is a full-service digital marketing agency.

Fred Reichheld is a fellow at Bain & Company, the creator of the Net Promoter System, and the bestselling author of several books on customer and employee loyalty, including *The Ultimate Question 2.0* (Harvard Business Review Press, 2011), with Rob Markey.

Omar Rodríguez-Vilá is a professor in the practice of marketing at the Goizueta Business School at Emory University and the academic director of education at its Business & Society Institute.

Jann Schwarz leads Marketplace Innovation and is the founder of the B2B Institute at LinkedIn.

Mimi Turner is the head of Marketplace Innovation and former head of EMEA & Latin America at the B2B Institute at LinkedIn.

Kimberly A. Whitler is the Frank M. Sands Sr. Associate Professor of Business Administration at the University of Virginia's Darden School of Business and a coauthor of *Athlete Brands*.

Annie Wilson is a senior lecturer of marketing at the Wharton School of the University of Pennsylvania. She is a coauthor of *The Growth Dilemma* (Harvard Business Review Press, 2025). She advises B2C and B2B companies across various industries on branding, marketing, and customer experience management.

Jonathan Z. Zhang is the Dr. Ajay Menon Professor in Business and an associate professor of marketing at Colorado State University. His scholarly work has been published in academic and management journals such as *Marketing Science, Journal of Marketing, Journal of the Academy of Marketing Science, Harvard Business Review, MIT Sloan Management Review,* and *California Management Review.*

Index